MICHAEL BARRY'S WAITROSE
recipes

as broadcast on Classic FM

Michael Barry's
Waitrose
Recipes

First published in 2000 by
Waitrose Limited
Bracknell, Berkshire, RG12 8YA
Produced and designed by
The Erskine Press
Banham, Norwich, NR16 2HW

Recipes by Michael Barry
Food for photography by The Banham Bakehouse, Norfolk
Food styling by Lesley de Boos
Photography © Andrew Perkins 2000
Designed by jack afrika Associates
Text copyright © Michael Barry 2000
This edition copyright © Waitrose Limited 2000

ISBN 0–9537983–0–5

Printed in Spain

Waitrose & Wine

Wine availability and price are correct at time of going to press. *Waitrose* wine departments have specialists to advise on wines and on any substitute should a particular wine not be available. Smaller *Waitrose* branches may stock a more limited selection of wines. Glasses are available for lending without charge. Please ask your local branch for details.

Waitrose Wine Direct

Waitrose Wine Direct is a home-delivery service. Wine lists also include some fine and rare 'Inner Cellar' wines not stocked in all branches. To find out more, free-phone 0800 188881 or write to *Waitrose Wine Direct*, Freepost (SW1647), Bracknell RG12 8HX or via www.waitrose.com

Waitrose Supermarkets

Waitrose was named 'Retailer of the Year' at the 1999 International Wine and Spirit Competition. The 'Best Supermarket Award' in the *'Which?'* Wine Guide Awards for 2000 was won by *Waitrose*, which was also voted, for the second year running, 'Organic Supermarket of the Year 1999/2000' by *'You'* magazine.

Waitrose & the Internet

Whether you are looking for recipe ideas for a dinner party, wine to be delivered to your door or even the latest copy of *Waitrose Food Illustrated*, www.waitrose.com is the site to visit. If you don't already have access to the internet, you can choose Waitrose.com as your internet service provider. Call into any branch of *Waitrose* to pick up a free CD or visit www.waitrose.com for more information.

Contents

Introduction

Ten thirty-five every weekday morning used to be a very special time on Henry Kelly's show on Classic FM. It was the time for the Waitrose recipe, ten minutes of music, banter and culinary wisdom, or crafty tips as they were more readily known. On Henry's programme there was always (and still is) a lot to listen out for: Irish philosophy, usually known as jokes, horse racing tips, usually best avoided, and Henry's genuine love of the beautiful music he plays. But the highlight was always, for me at least, the Waitrose recipe spot. They were usually done live, and therefore neither of us knew for certain where the next line lay. Nor did our long suffering and superb producer, Jane Jones. Now a star in her own right, Jane used to guide us through the pitfalls of our own ad-libbing with patient good humour.

There was, of course, always the recipe itself. A series of starters, main courses and on Fridays a pudding, that not only was broadcast to over a million people every day, but was also supplied free to thousands more who wrote or phoned in. What I've chosen here is around a hundred of our, and your, favourites, taken from those daily slots, all easily cooked and prepared and with ingredients you can find at your local Waitrose store. I have also added a few musical notes when the dish brought back a special memory or thought from the happy days where music and food seemed such natural partners. I hope you enjoy them both.

Soups and Starters

There was a time in the not too distant past when a dinner party might have seen five courses that included a soup and a starter. In those days the starter might have been called an entrée, but these days it is much more a case of 'either/or' to start a meal. With more and more people, including me, anxious to eat healthily and watch the 'avoirdupois', lighter meals are an inevitable trend. It doesn't mean, however, that you have to sacrifice taste or variety. It's in this area of the overture that the balanced concert that every meal should be, has developed more variety than any other.

I've selected a wide range in both areas of choice. Some are crafty versions of great classical traditions, like the Cream of Watercress Soup, or the Pâté of Salmon. Others are in the modern idiom, with flavours like goat's cheese or the olive oil and basil savours of the Provençal *Soupe au Pistou*. I hope you will agree that they all make the kind of beginning to a meal that lifts and whets the appetite, as well as being satisfying in their own right.

Cauliflower and Cheddar cheese soup

This soup is perfect for lunch on an autumn or winter's day. It is warm, filling and tastes marvellous, as it combines one of the most classic of mixtures, cauliflower and cheese, in a novel way. The last minute addition of the raw cauliflower gives the whole soup a really interesting texture so don't be tempted to leave it out.

INGREDIENTS
Serves 4

1 medium onion, peeled

175 g/6 oz potatoes

450 g/1 lb fresh cauliflower

1 tbsp sunflower oil

850 ml/1½ pints hot chicken stock (a stock cube will do) or boiling water

½ tsp white sugar

A good pinch salt and pepper

175 g/6 oz good mature cheddar cheese, grated

1 Chop the onion and potatoes.

2 Divide the cauliflower into small florets and put a quarter to one side.

3 Heat the oil in a large saucepan and when it's hot, fry the onion very gently until translucent. Add the potatoes.

4 Give it a stir, pour in the boiling water or chicken stock, add the sugar, salt and pepper (you may not need to add much salt if using a stock cube as they can be quite salty already) and cook the potatoes and onions for about ten minutes.

5 Add three quarters of the cauliflower and cook until tender – about ten more minutes. Pour it into a blender or food processor with the remaining raw florets and whiz for a few seconds. If you don't have a machine, push the cooked vegetables through a sieve to purée them, chop the remaining raw florets very finely and stir them into the purée.

6 Pour the soup back into the saucepan over a low heat and stir in the grated cheddar until the soup is streaked with gold!

7 Serve with granary or crusty French bread.

DRINK RECOMMENDATION

A crisp, dry, fresh white would do the trick here, cleansing the palate between mouthfuls.
Le Pujalet 1998 Vin de Pays du Gers – £3.39

Opposite: ***Soupe au Pisto***
Broad bean soup with chives
Cauliflower and cheddar cheese soup

Broad bean soup with chives

Broad beans are at their peak in June and it may well be you wish to do nothing but steam them and eat them with lightly herbed butter and some good brown bread. I could hardly blame you but when you've had enough of that particular self-indulgence, try making them into this delicious light green soup. Though it's not fashionable to say so, you can also make a delicious version with frozen broad beans, but do not admit it!

INGREDIENTS
Serves 4

1 large floury potato, approximately 225 g/8 oz

1 medium onion

225 g/8 oz broad beans de-podded (or frozen)

850 ml/1½ pints of water

2 tbsp cooking oil

1 tbsp chopped fresh chives or 1 tsp freeze-dried

25 g/1 oz butter

1 Peel the potato and onion and rough chop. Fry gently in the oil in a large saucepan with the broad beans. Season generously and add the water.

2 Cook, lightly covered, for approximately 15 minutes. If you are using frozen beans cook the potato first then add the beans for 5 minutes only. The beans should still be green, not khaki.

3 Pour the mixture into a food processor or liquidiser – you may need to do it in two batches – and process until completely smooth. Add the chopped chives and the butter and stir in thoroughly before serving.

4 Serve with crusty French bread.

Cream of watercress soup

This soup, known as soupe cressonière, is one of the great classic dishes of French cuisine. In certain great house traditions of English cookery it also puts in a frequent appearance, but often we forget how simple and delicious it is to make. Fresh raw watercress has a lovely peppery flavour. It is a good idea to keep a little of the cress aside to purée in with the cooked soup at the very end to give it a little extra punch. For this, if you have no fresh stock, it's worth buying a carton of the ready made variety for flavour.

INGREDIENTS
Serves 4

350 g/12 oz potatoes

225 g/8 oz onion

25 g/1 oz each cooking oil and butter

2 large bunches fresh watercress

1.2 litres/2 pints of chicken stock or water

55 g/2 oz double cream

1 Peel the potatoes and onions and cut into cubes. Fry these gently in the oil and butter until the onion is translucent.

2 Wash the cress thoroughly and put aside a third of one bunch. Add the remaining cress to the potato and onion mixture and turn in the butter for a minute. Season generously, add the stock or water (water produces a lighter, clearer tasting soup, stock a richer one) and simmer for 12 to 15 minutes until the potato is completely tender. Do not cook for longer than this or the cress will lose its impact.

3 Put into a food processor or liquidiser with the retained third of the bunch of cress and process until a smooth purée. You may need to do this in two batches. Return to the saucepan and check for seasoning and stir in the double cream. Serve immediately with small croutons or toasted slivered almonds floated on top.

Soupe au pistou

This is a vegetable soup made with fresh beans and flavoured with a marvellous basil and cheese concoction known in Southern France as pistou. Pistou is a close relative of the Italian pesto sauce that is so popular now.

INGREDIENTS
Serves 4

225 g/8 oz shelled or frozen broad beans

115 g/4 oz each:–
Onion
Carrots
Fresh or frozen peas
Celery
Tomatoes

4 tbsp olive oil

Salt and pepper

850 ml/1¹/₂ pints water or stock

PISTOU

25 g/1 oz fresh basil leaves

1 tbsp olive oil

1 clove of garlic

55 g/2 oz Pine nuts

55 g/2 oz gruyère cheese

1   Peel and dice all the soup vegetables. You can substitute or add to the mixture if it suits you – courgettes, potatoes and 1 cm/¹/₂ in lengths of French beans are all acceptable.

2   Gently sauté all the vegetables except the tomatoes in 1 tablespoon of the olive oil. Season generously with salt and pepper and add the water or stock. Bring to the boil and simmer for 12 minutes.

3   Meanwhile, to make the Pistou, put the remaining oil, the clove of garlic, the pine nuts and the basil leaves into a food processor or liquidiser and purée till almost smooth. You may need to add a little more oil or a tablespoon of water to make the mixture work smoothly. Add the grated gruyère and process again until thoroughly blended.

4   Finally add the chopped tomatoes to the soup; allow to simmer one more minute. Serve the pistou separately: diners stir a spoonful into their soup before eating.

Paté of salmon

With fresh salmon these days cheaper than cod, this is not nearly as luxurious to make, as it seems to eat. It can be easily made the evening before and improves with a little rest overnight for the flavours to blend. Serve it with brown or granary toast and a quarter of lemon to squeeze over for each diner. If you would like a modern serving style, line small ramekins with oiled cling film and chill the pâté in those. They will turn out effortlessly and should be served on a bed of frisée lettuce elegantly arranged on individual plates.

INGREDIENTS
Serves 4

450 g/1 lb fresh salmon

½ tsp salt

1 lemon

4 peppercorns

55 g/2 oz butter

55 g/2 oz low fat fromage frais

1 tbsp fresh or 1 tsp dried dill

1 The salmon, which can be either cutlets or a piece, should be put into a pan of cold water with the salt, a quarter of the lemon, and the peppercorns. Bring it gently to the boil and allow it to cook for 3 to 4 minutes and switch the heat off. Leave the salmon, with a lid on, in the water for an hour to cool and finish cooking.

2 Take it out of the water, skin and bone it, and mash the flesh with a fork or in a food processor until it's well crumbled but not totally smooth.

3 Melt the butter and add with the fromage frais, the finely chopped dill and the juice from the remaining lemon. Check for seasoning, it may need a little more salt, pack it into an attractive soufflé dish and chill for at least three hours. You can, if you like, pour a little more melted butter over the top to seal it. Then it will keep for up to four days uncut.

DRINK RECOMMENDATION

Chardonnay is a safe bet with salmon. Choose a crisp one to match the lemon and peppercorns.

Chablis 1997 Gaec des Réugnis – £7.99

Lemony eggs with shrimps

This recipe is derived from an Egyptian way of cooking eggs and tastes wonderfully creamy and fresh. I added the shrimps, though whether they should be called prawns is a matter of some debate. It's nice with the little brown shrimps often sold potted, or for special occasions with those lovely big tropical tiger prawns. Either way, I serve it as a hot hors d'oeuvre with thin brown toast and a slice of lemon on the side.

INGREDIENTS
Serves 4

8 free range eggs

25 g/1 oz butter

1 small clove garlic, crushed

Salt and freshly ground black pepper

Juice of a lemon

115 g/4 oz prawns, cooked and peeled or potted shrimps

1 Use a large, solid pan for this. Thin-based ones mean the butter and eggs heat unevenly, so part isn't cooked and the rest is burnt.

2 Crack the eggs into a bowl and lightly beat them together. Melt the butter in the saucepan, then add the eggs and scramble them gently until they are soft but not quite set.

3 Add the crushed garlic and season the eggs with salt and pepper. Just before they set, add the lemon juice. This has an extraordinary effect. It stops the eggs setting and makes them go creamy. They also turn a pale, lemony gold colour.

4 Take them off the heat immediately and stir in the shrimps. They are already cooked and the heat from the eggs is enough to warm them through. Pile this wonderful pink and pale gold mixture onto toast or, if you are serving this as a starter, heap it into ramekins. A small sprinkle of parsley is very decorative.

MUSIC RECOMMENDATION

The dish has an Egyptian origin and the most famous piece to share that distinction is the opera *Aida* that Verdi wrote for the inauguration of the new opera house in Cairo, to mark the opening of the Suez Canal in 1869. There are many much loved pieces in the monumental work, but my favourite would be the triumphal march *Ritorna Vincitor* with those wonderful trumpet fanfares.

Crafty pepperonata with goat's cheese

This is an Italian-style salad which, in its original form, required a lot of complex grilling and peeling of the peppers. This is to get rid of the rather waxy outside coating but the crafty method here allows that same coating to be cooked off without too much fiddling about. The contrast between the sweetness of the peppers and the clear-tasting creaminess of the cheese makes this an outstanding first course or, in larger quantities, a light lunch. A lot of very good goat's cheese is now made in the UK, in many forms including the small rounds that are ideal for this dish. Check your cheese counter.

INGREDIENTS
Serves 4

700 g/1 lb 9 oz sweet peppers, mixed colours

2 tablespoons olive oil

1 clove of garlic

Salt and pepper

Juice of 1 lemon

85 g/3 oz round of fresh, white goat's cheese

1 tbsp chopped parsley

1 Halve the peppers, making sure you have at least two colours, and remove the seeds. Slice across into quarter inch strips. Heat the oil in a frying pan which will take all the peppers.

2 Peel and finely chop the garlic and add to the oil. Immediately add the pepper slices and turn over a medium to high heat for 2 to 3 minutes. Season with salt and pepper, turn the heat down and allow the peppers to cook gently for about 10 minutes until they are just beginning to caramelise. Squeeze the lemon juice over them, turn thoroughly and allow to cool.

3 Cut the goat's cheese into four slices across the round and dip one side of each slice into the chopped parsley.

4 To serve, place the pepper pieces in an attractive dish or individual dishes and arrange the sliced goat's cheese, parsley side up, on top. The peppers should be completely cool and can be stored in the fridge (before adding the cheese) for up to 12 hours.

5 Serve with crusty country bread.

DRINK RECOMMENDATION

Both capsicum and goat's cheese are crying out for Sauvignon Blanc. The crispness and earthy green fruit will bring the dish's flavours together.

Springfield Special Cuvée
Sauvignon Blanc 1998/99
Robertson – £6.99

Mini smoked salmon and parsley quiches

To make this dish you need what is known in Britain as a mini Yorkshire pudding tin, a baking tin with four dents in it about 3 inches across and about an inch deep. We tend to use them for making individual Yorkshire puddings but in Europe they're used for making mini sized quiches or tarts. Or you could be even smarter and buy ready made canapé cases. Either way the filling of smoked salmon and parsley is extraordinarily pretty and delicate, and these are quite easily made and good enough for a special occasion.

INGREDIENTS
Makes four individual quiches or 16–20 canapés

225 g/8 oz shortcrust pastry or 20 ready-made canapé cases

150 g/6 oz smoked salmon (off-cut pieces will do very well)

55 g/2 oz parsley

1 egg plus 1 egg yolk

150 ml/¹⁄₄ pint double cream

Pinch of nutmeg

1 Pre-heat the oven to 220°C/425°F/gas mark 7/top of the Aga roasting oven

2 Divide the pastry into four and either roll out each piece and line the tart tins or divide into four and press the pastry into the tin until it fills the four indentations neatly. Cut the smoked salmon into small pieces about the size of a fingernail and divide between the pastry shells.

3 Chop the parsley. Beat the egg and egg yolk together with the cream. Sprinkle the parsley over the salmon and pour the egg and cream mixture through a sieve into the tart cases. If pouring into canapé cases it would be better to sieve the mixture into a jug and pour or spoon it on. Sprinkle with a little salt and pepper and the pinch of nutmeg.

4 Bake for 25 minutes until the pastry is lightly browned and the filling cooked and risen; 12–15 minutes for the canapés. Serve hot or warm.

DRINK RECOMMENDATION

Any gently oaked Chardonnay.

Lindemans Bin 65 Chardonnay, 1998 South Eastern Australia – £4.99

Baked avocado with crab

We tend to think of avocados as salad ingredients to eat cold but in the land of their origin, the highlands of Central America, they were often, and still are, eaten hot. It's important to get avocados at the right point for successful cooking: when they are ripe enough to give slightly to the touch but not in any sense overripe or discoloured, because if they are they will collapse while heating. Frozen crabmeat is fine for this dish, but tinned crab isn't so good. This makes a really luxurious starter.

INGREDIENTS
Serves 4

2 large avocados, ripe but not too soft

3 spring onions

175 g/6 oz cooked white crabmeat

4 tbsp mayonnaise

1 tsp dried red pepper flakes (or a dried salad seasoning, which includes red pepper flakes)

Juice of 1 lemon

1 Pre-heat the oven to 190°C/375°F/gas mark 5/middle of Aga roasting oven

2 Split the avocados and remove the stones. Rub the avocados with the cut side of the lemon to stop them going brown.

3 Finely chop the onions. Mix together the onions, crab, mayonnaise and the dried red pepper flakes. Pour half the lemon juice over the avocados and the remaining juice on the crab mixture.

4 Fill the hollow of each avocado with a mound of the crab mixture. Cover with a butter paper or oiled greaseproof paper or foil. Place the pears on a baking dish and put into the oven for 15 minutes or until the avocados and filling are hot but not collapsed. It could take up to 20 minutes depending on the size of the fruit.

5 Serve hot in bowls to keep the avocados and their contents upright.

Wild mushroom salad

I first tasted this salad after a mushroom-gathering session in the Hampshire woods. It was a revelation both for its taste and as a reminder of our 'wild' resources. Although the recipe requires wild mushrooms, it is now possible to make it with some of the new varieties of cultivated mushrooms available on the greengrocery shelves. Try oyster or chestnut mushrooms, which are a halfway house between the real wild ones and old-fashioned domesticated ones. The salad is a smashing accompaniment to simply-grilled meat but also quite nice as a course on its own. If you are picking your own mushrooms do be very careful to avoid any poisonous varieties.

INGREDIENTS
Serves 4

450 g/1 lb wild mushrooms, washed well to remove any grit but not peeled

1 chopped clove garlic

2 tbsp olive oil

2 tbsp lemon juice

1/2 tsp caster sugar

Lettuce, sorrel, rocket or radish leaves (for the salad base)

1 tsp each chopped parsley and chives

Seasoning

DRINK RECOMMENDATION

Barrel fermented Chardonnays such as a white Burgundy.

1 Slice the mushrooms into attractive shapes. Sauté them with the chopped garlic in 1 tablespoon of the oil for 2 minutes. Do not let them burn.

2 Place them in a bowl and, while still warm, toss with the remaining oil, adding the lemon juice pre-mixed with the caster sugar until this has dissolved. Season, then cool.

3 On individual plates, shred the lettuce with the sorrel or rocket leaves and sprinkle with the herbs. Spoon the mushrooms on top. Don't let it hang around long, although you can leave the mushrooms to marinate for a couple of hours before putting them on the greens.

Blinis with sour cream and caviar

The *blini* is the classic Russian pancake. Traditionally it was made from a yeast-raised batter which took quite a long time to work. This crafty version uses baking powder, which doesn't get quite such a spectacular lift, but it takes about eleven hours less time! They're a savoury pancake meant to be eaten with sour cream, melted butter and caviar. Real caviar comes a bit steep these days in or out of Russia, so I suggest you try them with the black lumpfish roe 'caviar' that's available on the delicatessen counter. Served like that, blinis make a spectacular first course to a grand dinner party. Properly, blinis are made with buckwheat – a grain grown widely in Eastern Europe. If you can't find buckwheat flour, which is sometimes available in health food shops, use a mixture of 50% wholemeal and 50% white self-raising flour.

INGREDIENTS
Serves 4

140 g/5 oz flour (see left)

1 tsp baking powder

½ tsp bicarbonate of soda

1 egg

Pinch of salt

Pinch of sugar

150 ml/¼ pint milk

3 tbsp live natural yoghurt

1 Beat the flour, baking powder, bicarbonate of soda, sugar, salt and egg together. Stir the milk and yoghurt together, add to the mixture and beat thoroughly.

2 Heat a large frying-pan, grease lightly, and place a tablespoon of the batter in the pan. Continue to place separate spoonfuls until you've got as many into the pan as possible. Each pancake should be about 6 cm/2½ inches across and will be quite thick. When they are golden on the bottom, after about 2 minutes, turn them over and cook for about another minute to a minute-and-a-half over a low to medium heat on the second side.

3 Keep the blinis on a warm plate in a warm place, a low oven is a good idea, and when they're all ready, serve two or three overlapped around a big tablespoon of sour cream topped with whatever caviar you can afford. If you don't fancy caviar of any sort, try a teaspoon of finely chopped fresh chives on the sour cream.

Pasta and Salads

Classical music may be rooted in tradition, but, in the matter of eating, our Classic FM audience made it very clear that as well as the old favourites, they were ready for the new lighter style of meals. We ran a free-phone recipe service so we could tell from the response which dishes really hit the spot. Anything with chocolate in it always did well and pies were popular, but pasta dishes and salads, especially meal salads, always scored.

In fact the availability of produce in these two areas is quite astonishing today. Five or six varieties of lettuce vie with the more 'fancy' greens of rocket or endive as a basis for salads. If it's tomatoes you are after, would you like huge *marmandes* or tiny plum, yellow fleshed or vine ripened? Perhaps it's pasta you prefer … fresh or dried? White, green or red? Herbed or egg or plain? And what about shape … the choice is endless, and exciting, and that's before you get to the matter of sauces.

So I'm offering here a selection of some of the more exciting, and possibly uncommon, salad and pasta dishes for which there was great response. It's not that I don't love an old fashioned tossed green salad, but try it in the form of coriander with mushrooms, or how about pasta with a blue cheese sauce. All the healthiness, all the flavour, with a twist.

Tabbouleh

Tabbouleh is a marvellous Middle Eastern salad. Its base is cracked wheat, which is now available in your supermarket along with many other exotic grains. Traditionally it's a salad served with cos lettuce leaves, which can be used as a kind of vegetable spoon to wrap around the tabbouleh mouthful by mouthful. However you eat it, it's a nutty, substantial salad that makes a good first course.

INGREDIENTS
Serves 4

115 g/4 oz Bulghur cracked wheat sometimes labelled Podghouri

300 ml/½ pint of warm water

55 g/2 oz parsley

A small handful of mint leaves

1 medium to large tomato

4 sticks of spring onion, trimmed

2 tbsp olive oil

1 tbsp lemon juice

1 Soak the wheat grains in the water. It may seem unlikely at first but they will absorb all the water and you may indeed need to add a little more to make the mixture barely moist.

2 Chop the herbs very finely and rough chop the tomato and trimmed spring onions. Mix all of these into the wheat after it has had a chance to stand for half an hour. Add the lemon juice and olive oil. Stir thoroughly and test for seasoning. It will certainly need a little salt.

3 The finished product should be golden, speckled with green and red from the herbs and tomato, and moist enough to spoon easily but not so wet that it has any running liquid. Serve in individual bowls with little gem or cos lettuce leaves arranged as a base.

Coriander and mushroom salad

This dish is a kind of *mushrooms à la grecque* with a little added spice. The idea originally came from Elizabeth David who is really the creative instigator of so much that's become good in modern British food. It makes a delicious starter on its own or a good foil for other dishes in a mixed hors d'oeuvre. It keeps well in the fridge; indeed, it may well improve with 24 hours for the flavours to blend.

INGREDIENTS
Serves 4

450 g/1 lb small, closed mushrooms

100 ml/3½ fl oz water

100 ml/3½ fl oz olive oil

50 ml/2 fl oz lemon juice (fresh or bottled)

1 clove garlic, chopped

1 bay leaf

1 tsp ground coriander

1 tbsp chopped coriander or celery leaf

Salt and pepper

1 Wash and trim the mushrooms but don't peel them. Bring the water, oil and lemon juice and the bay leaf to the boil and add the mushrooms and garlic. Simmer for 5 minutes.

2 Add the ground coriander, and season. Pour the mixture into a basin and leave to cool. Drain the mushrooms and place in a serving dish, reserving the marinade.

3 Sprinkle over the chopped coriander and moisten with 4 tablespoons of the sieved marinade. Serve well chilled.

MUSIC RECOMMENDATION

The Greek connection here suggests part of Gluck's lovely opera, set in classical Greece, *Orpheus and Eurydice*. I especially like the hauntingly lovely aria 'Che faro' which although sung by Orpheus was written for what we think of as a woman's range today and is often sung by a contralto.

American potato salad

The best potatoes to use for this, although it's an American idea, are new Jersey Royals, or any salad variety of potato – Fir Apple Pink, Kipfler or Charlotte. They all stay firm when cooked – they do not disintegrate into mush, which is crucial! Americans eat potato salad with frankfurters, coleslaw, grilled meat and so on. It is also very nice with a couple of other salads as a light and vegetarian meal. The important thing to remember is that it's meant to be eaten warm. Trust me.

INGREDIENTS
Serves 4

450 g/1 lb new, salad potatoes

1 bunch spring onions

25 g/1 oz fresh parsley

4 tbsp of mayonnaise – home-made is ideal

2 tbsp fromage frais or Greek yoghurt

1 tsp French mustard

Good pinch salt and pepper

1 tbsp lemon juice or cider vinegar

1 Scrub but do not peel the potatoes. Cut them into even sized pieces and put them into a pan of cold water with a big pinch of salt, bring to the boil and cook until the potatoes are just tender. It should take between eight and ten minutes, but this depends on the size of the potatoes.

2 When they are cooked, drain them and cut them into pieces roughly the size of dice. Meanwhile trim and chop the spring onions and do the same with the parsley. Mix the fromage frais or yoghurt with the mayonnaise and mustard.

3 When the potatoes have stopped steaming, sprinkle them with salt and a tablespoon of lemon juice or cider vinegar. Do this while the potatoes are still hot, as they will absorb that sharp edge and saltiness.

4 Toss the potatoes in the mayonnaise and fromage frais mixed together, add the spring onion and parsley and turn it all until blended. Serve warm.

If you have never eaten hot potato salad, you are in for a treat! You can of course let it cool. Either way it is delicious with a marvellous fresh texture.

Tomato salad with basil dressing

At many times of the year vine ripened tomatoes become available, and at last we have varieties chosen and grown for their flavour and not just their uniformity of shape. Try and find the large *Marmande* tomatoes for this particular salad as their texture as well as their flavour make it more interesting. An alternative is to use the marble sized cherry tomatoes, which also have an intensity of flavour, and to just cut them in half. Fresh basil, the perfect herb for tomatoes, is always available now.

INGREDIENTS
Serves 4

450 g/1 lb tomatoes, large or small

25 g/1 oz fresh basil

3 spring onions

1 tbsp olive oil

3 tbsp salad oil

1 tbsp red wine vinegar

Splash of lemon juice

1/2 tsp sugar

1/2 tsp salt

1 Wash and slice the tomatoes into 5 mm/¼ in thick slices and lay them in an attractive pattern in a shallow china dish. If using cherry tomatoes, halve these and place in the same sort of container.

2 Rinse the basil leaves and trim the spring onions and cut into 1 cm/½ in lengths. Put these into a liquidiser or food processor with the oils, vinegar, lemon juice, sugar and salt. Process until it becomes a smooth thick green purée.

3 Pour this over the tomatoes and leave to marinate for at least half an hour – up to 2 or 3 hours in the fridge is fine. Decorate with a few reserved basil leaves and serve with crisp French bread to wipe the plates.

DRINK RECOMMENDATION

A gentle, herbaceous white would be excellent. Try a top Soave such as

Soave Classico DOC 1997/98 Vigneto Colombara, Zenato – £4.95

Iceberg lettuce with blue cheese dressing

I first came across this dish in New York where Classic FM has a sister station. It was served in a steak house as a first course. I'm bound to say that the steak house lived up to the American reputation for huge portions. They served nearly half a large lettuce in a chunk to be eaten with a knife and fork. While this is a slight modification in presentation, what I have tried to maintain is the terrific combination of crisp greens and a piquant creamy dressing. It's still a substantial dish.

INGREDIENTS
Serves 4

1 large iceberg lettuce

DRESSING:

115 g/4 oz not too expensive blue cheese, e.g. Danish or bleu d'Auvergne

Juice of a lemon

¹/₂ tsp each salt and sugar

2 tbsp salad oil

150 ml/¹/₄ pint milk

1 Without separating the lettuce, wash and trim it cutting out the stalk as much as possible. Using a stainless knife cut it into quarters (a bread knife is good for this).

2 Cut each quarter in half again and arrange on plates two slices to a portion. Put all the dressing ingredients into a processor or liquidiser, crumbling the cheese and whiz until smooth.

3 Just before you want to eat, spoon all the dressing over the lettuce and serve.

DRINK RECOMMENDATION

Blue cheese is lethal to any wine

MUSIC RECOMMENDATION

Robust food like this needs robust music. What more appropriate to an American dish than some quintessentially American music, John Philip Sousa's great march *The Stars and Stripes For Ever*.

Penne with courgette and herb sauce

A lovely quick-to-make recipe, ideal to serve with the bulky pasta like penne, spirals or snail shells. The idea in Italy is that the big pasta pieces soak up and carry more of the sauce. The dried mushrooms in the recipe; the Italians use a kind called 'porcini'; add lots of flavour intensity and are quite important for the balance of the dish. They are expensive but you can buy them in quite small packets and a little goes a long way.

INGREDIENTS
Serves 4

350 g/12 oz penne or other dried pasta

350 g/12 oz courgettes

50 ml/2 fl oz olive oil

1 finely chopped onion

1 tsp chopped garlic

1 tsp freeze dried oregano

1 tsp freeze dried basil or a few fresh leaves, shredded

½ tsp dried thyme

25 g/1 oz dried mushrooms, soaked in hot water for 10 minutes

4 tbsp tomato purée

175 ml/6 fl oz water

Parmesan to serve

1 Cook the pasta in plenty of boiling, salted water until *al dente* (about 10 minutes).

2 Meanwhile, wash and trim the courgettes, slice them into rounds the thickness of pound coins and fry briskly in the oil with the onion for 3 minutes.

3 Add the garlic, oregano, basil, thyme and dried mushrooms along with a splash of their soaking liquid. Add the tomato purée and the water, check the seasoning and stir until it is well mixed.

4 Simmer for 3 minutes and pour over the cooked, drained pasta. Serve in a big shallow bowl with Parmesan and perhaps a little black pepper and with more fresh chopped basil sprinkled over.

MUSIC RECOMMENDATION

Such Italian dishes need Italian music, but, to ring the changes, not by an Italian composer. Italy has inspired many not born on her shores. After his disastrous marriage, the Russian composer Tchaikovsky travelled to Italy to recuperate. He was in Rome for the carnival in 1880 and the liveliness and love of life he saw inspired him to write one of his most buoyant pieces, the *Capriccio Italien*. It's full of sunshine and the most lilting of melodies.

Pasta with spring vegetables

This is a dish adapted from the restaurant, Chez Panisse, in Berkeley, California, famous for the amalgamation of European, Mexican and West Coast American food. This vegetarian pasta dish makes a perfect light lunch or a very interesting starter served in smaller quantities. If you change the butter for one of the non-dairy spreads, it also makes a delicious vegan meal.

INGREDIENTS
Serves 6

450 g/1 lb very fine pasta or spaghetti, fresh or dried

12 stalks of asparagus

350 g/12 oz fresh peas, shelled (frozen will do)

350 g/12 oz broad beans, shelled (frozen will do)

115 g/4 oz butter, softened

A good handful of basil leaves

A good handful of flat leaf parsley

3 tbsp olive oil

1 clove of garlic, chopped

1 Put the pasta into a large pan of boiling water with a pinch of salt and a drop of olive oil. Allow to cook for 3 minutes, remove from the heat, and put the lid on. Leave to stand for 6 minutes if the pasta is dried or drain immediately if it is fresh.

2 Trim and discard any hard woody parts of the asparagus then cut into 1 cm/$\frac{1}{2}$ in lengths and boil in a minimum of water with the fresh peas and beans for approximately 5 minutes. If using frozen vegetables, add them after the asparagus is cooked. Leave to stand for 2 minutes and then drain.

3 Mix the butter with a handful each of chopped basil and parsley leaves. Put the olive oil into a large pan and add the garlic and the blanched vegetables. Allow to heat through. Add the drained pasta and the herb butter and toss until thoroughly mixed.

4 Grate a little Parmesan cheese over it.

Three bean salad

Around Christmas salad vegetables are not at their best, but it is possible to make really marvellous salads out of other vegetables and in fact even out of dried vegetables and pulses. This three bean salad can be made with store cupboard ingredients with a few herbs added and a really zesty dressing to give it some kick. It's delicious served as a starter, but it's also very nice as part of a buffet or to go with grilled meats. You can vary the ingredients to suit the kind of beans that you like or indeed can find. (Do try and mix the colours and the sizes. I've suggested including some fresh green beans in this version to go with the white and red of the haricot and red kidney beans, but you can do it all with dried beans including something like pinto or black beans for a colour variation.) Dress the salad at least half an hour before you're going to eat it so that the beans can absorb the flavours. If you haven't got time to soak and cook the beans, you can use some tinned varieties, but do rinse them thoroughly first.

INGREDIENTS
Serves 4

175 g/6 oz each dried haricot and red kidney beans

225 g/8 oz green French beans

4 tbsp olive oil

2 tbsp lemon juice

1 tsp each sugar and salt

Small bunch of spring onions

25 g/1 oz parsley

1 Soak the two dried beans overnight or for at least 6 hours in plenty of water. Put in a saucepan and cover with water but don't add any salt. Bring to the boil and boil for 10 minutes. Drain, re-cover with water and simmer for an hour to an hour-and-a-half until the beans are tender but not coming to pieces.

2 Cook the green beans, which should be cut into 1 cm/½ in lengths, for 8 minutes. Mix the dressing ingredients together, chop the parsley, trim then roughly chop the spring onions .

3 Drain the beans and mix them together gently in a serving dish. Shake or whisk the dressing ingredients together and pour over the beans while they're still warm.

4 Stir in the chopped spring onion and sprinkle the parsley over the top and leave to marinate in the fridge for at least 30 minutes and ideally for 2 hours. Give them a little stir before you serve them to make sure that the dressing hasn't all drained to the bottom.

Baked macaroni Campagnese

Pasta is cooked in a lot of other ways in the Italian Campagna than simply boiling in water and serving with a sauce. It's used in bakes and pies and gratins. This is one of the nicest and simplest. I once saw Valentina Harris do a dish rather like this in a cookery demonstration in Britain and noticed that of all the dishes left backstage afterwards this one went the quickest. The sauce here is a modern version of the traditional Italian tomato sauce. It uses the small cherry tomatoes that are as prevalent in the south of Italy as they are in our stores.

INGREDIENTS
Serves 6

450 g/1 lb macaroni, straight or 'elbows'

1 clove of garlic

1 bunch of spring onions

4 tbsp olive oil

700 g/1 lb 9 oz cherry tomatoes

225 g/8 oz each of mozzarella and fontina cheese (450 g/1 lb of either will do)

1 handful of fresh basil

2 tbsp grated parmesan

1 Pre-heat the oven to 180°C/350°F/gas mark 4/bottom of Aga roasting oven.

2 Bring a pan of water to the boil with a pinch of salt and a drop of oil, add the pasta and cook for 3–4 minutes. Cover, switch off the heat and leave for 7 minutes while you make the tomato sauce.

3 Peel and chop the garlic, trim and finely chop the spring onions and cook those in the olive oil for 2–3 minutes until golden. Add the cherry tomatoes, cut into quarters, season generously and simmer for 10 minutes.

4 Cut the cheese or cheeses into 1 cm/½ in dice.

5 Drain the pasta, mix it with the tomato sauce and stir in the basil, finely chopped. Season generously. Add the diced cheese, off the heat, and pour the mixture into a gratin dish. Sprinkle the top with the parmesan. This sometimes has some fresh breadcrumbs mixed with it, but it should be a light, not a heavy, crusted coating.

6 Bake in a medium oven for 20–30 minutes until bubbling and golden. Serve as a dish on its own.

Real spaghetti bolognaise

This is a serious version of an authentic bolognaise sauce. Of all the dishes of international cooking, this is probably the most abused, but in its original form it was so good it inspired all the inadequate copies. It's much richer than the one you'll be used to and is representative of the very rich and quite luxurious cooking style for which Bologna is famous in Italy. This sauce is also a great basis for a superb lasagne, layered with pasta sheets and béchamel sauce.

INGREDIENTS
Serves 4

450 g/1 lb lean minced beef

115 g/4 oz chicken livers

2 tbsp olive oil

1 clove of garlic

1 small chopped onion

2 carrots, peeled and grated

400 g/14 oz tin chopped Italian tomatoes

2 tbsp concentrated tomato purée

1/2 tsp dried thyme

1 tsp each dried oregano and basil

350 g/1 lb spaghetti

2 tbsp double cream

1 Fry the beef and the chicken livers, which should also be roughly chopped, in the oil until they are lightly browned. Add the garlic and onion, chopped as finely as possible, and continue to cook for another 2 to 3 minutes.

2 Add the grated carrot and the tinned tomatoes, bring to the boil and stir in the tomato purée. If the sauce is too thick at this stage, add half a cup of water. Add the herbs and season generously. Leave a wooden spoon in the pan and cover with a lid. Simmer as gently as possible for 30 minutes.

3 Cook the pasta in plenty of boiling salted water until *al dente* then drain. Just before serving stir the double cream into the bolognaise sauce. Put the drained spaghetti into individual serving bowls and pour the sauce over the top. Grated parmesan cheese and freshly ground black pepper are the traditional accompaniments.

DRINK RECOMMENDATION

It must be a well rounded Italian.
Barbera d'Asti 1997
Araldica – £4.29

Poultry and Game

Over the last few years poultry has overtaken all other meat as the nation's favourite. There seem to be many reasons for this apart from the health scares over beef; the trend was established long before BSE appeared on the horizon. Firstly the question of taste is involved, especially the taste for lighter food which poultry in particular provides. Animal welfare and the increasing availability of free-range poultry have helped. I think this does matter both for humanitarian reasons and for the texture and flavour difference on the plate, so do look out for the free-range labels if you can.

Secondly there is the general issue of health and the bad press red meat has been getting in general. Here poultry and game with their lower fat content, particularly saturated fat, win hands down. Last but not least is the effort that has been put in to make these meats more user friendly. Chicken and turkey as well as duck are sold in convenient portions, often pre-seasoned or prepared for the grill; breast steaks, mince, spatchcocked poussins, all help make buying and cooking that much easier. It's not surprising then our tastes have changed, but does it explain why chicken tikka masala has become the favourite British dish? If not perhaps we will have to look at how good poultry is to eat. I hope I've brought you a few new ideas in these recipes, including a traditional Barry family dish that could just oust the tikka … check out the quail recipe.

Cold lemon roast chicken with tarragon sauce

This is my favourite way of roasting a chicken and a great holiday recipe as you can cook it in advance or take it on a picnic. When the bird cools, it is the most succulent chicken you have ever eaten! Use a free-range chicken if you can get it – the flavour is even more pronounced.

INGREDIENTS
Serves 4

1.6–1.8 kg/3½–4 lb oven-ready chicken

1 lemon

½ tsp each ground bayleaves, garlic salt and paprika

FOR THE HERB SAUCE:

140 g/5 oz fromage frais

1 heaped tbsp each chopped fresh tarragon and fresh basil

1 tbsp lemon juice

½ tsp salt

½ tsp sugar

1 Pre-heat the oven to 190°C/375°F/gas mark 5/bottom of the Aga roasting oven.

2 Put the chicken into an ovenproof dish into which it fits comfortably. Cut the lemon in half and put half inside the chicken as a stuffing. Squeeze the other half over the chicken and mix all the seasonings together. Sprinkle them all over the chicken.

3 Butter a couple of pieces of foil, or use butter papers, cover the chicken with them and put the bird in an oven for twenty minutes per 450 g/1 lb, plus twenty minutes.

4 Twenty minutes before the end of the cooking time, remove the foil to allow the skin to brown. Check with a skewer in the thickest part of the thigh that the juices run clear. If at all pink, cook for another quarter of an hour and test again.

5 Let the chicken cool in the dish then cut into serving pieces and chill until you're ready to serve. (You can serve this the conventional way…hot with all the trimmings and gravy made from the pan juices.)

6 To make the herb sauce simply mix the sauce ingredients together and serve in a sauce-boat with the chicken.

DRINK RECOMMENDATION

A rich, honeyed, oaked white with gentle flavours is worth splashing out for. The broad tropical flavours of Semillon work a treat.

Chateau Tahbilk Marsanne 1997/98 Victoria – £6.99

Poulet à l'ancienne

À l'ancienne is what the French call the whole-grain old-fashioned mustard, the kind that is sold in big pottery jars. It has a lovely pungent flavour, and although it doesn't have the eye-stinging quality of English mustard, it is definitely not mild! These days you can also buy it in smaller quantities in glass jars, though the flavour is just as strong. It colours and flavours the sauce just cutting its richness.

INGREDIENTS
Serves 4

1 tbsp oil

25 g/1 oz butter

4 boneless chicken breasts

1 cup of chicken stock or water

1 tsp cornflour

150 ml/¼ pint single cream

1 tbsp moutarde à l'ancienne

1 In a large frying pan, heat the butter in the oil. Put in the chicken breasts and sauté them skin side down for five minutes. Don't be tempted to add more fat: the skin contains fat and that comes out as the skin browns. Turn them over and sauté for another 5 to 6 minutes.

2 Pour in the cup of stock or water and simmer gently for another 12 to 15 minutes until the chicken is cooked through. When they're done, put the chicken breasts onto warm plates.

3 Mix the cornflour into the single cream, and pour the cream and mustard into the pan. Stir and bring it to the boil. The mustard helps to thicken the sauce with the cornflour, and the sauce turns a wonderful golden colour, with bite and texture from the mustard grains.

4 Pour it all over the chicken and serve at once. I love this with mashed potato, a taste my Irish colleague Henry Kelly has been known to share.

DRINK RECOMMENDATION

A lovely match for pepper and mustard sauces is the bright fruity
Waitrose Beaujolais
1998 – £4.49

Grilled spring chicken with grapefruit

The spring chickens referred to here are the old fashioned term for what are often called poussins these days. However, there is a difference in that poussins are delicious fully grown birds of a small species, and spring chickens are, as the name suggests, tender young birds from a regular species. Either way you need small birds for this dish full of quite unexpected flavours.

INGREDIENTS
Serves 4

2 x 750 g/1 lb 10 oz spring chickens, cut in half

FOR THE MARINADE:

4 tbsp grapeseed oil

1 tbsp grapefruit or lemon juice

1 tsp salt

1 tsp each ground ginger and milled pepper

1 clove of garlic, crushed

1 tbsp flower honey

TO GARNISH:

2 grapefruits, knife-segmented

1 tbsp roughly chopped coriander leaves

1 tbsp roughly chopped flat-leafed parsley

1 tbsp snipped chives

2 pieces preserved stem ginger, finely sliced

1 Have your butcher halve the chickens for you and chop away most of the backbone.

2 Mix all the ingredients for the marinade in a large non-metallic bowl. Leave the halved chickens in the marinade for 2 hours or more, or overnight in the fridge. Pre-heat the grill to a high heat.

3 Lightly brush the grill pan with oil. (This goes well on the barbecue.) Set the pan about 15 cm/6 in from the heat and grill the chicken halves, skin side up first, for 3–4 minutes. Turn them and cook for a similar length of time the other side. Lower the heat and continue to grill them, turning at 5 minute intervals, until they are brown, succulent and to your liking – depending on their size and on your particular grill, this will take 12–14 minutes overall. The honey will caramelise a little, which is intended.

4 Just before serving, arrange 3 or 4 grapefruit segments on top of each chicken half. Put back under the grill. Let them speckle with brown, sprinkle with fresh herbs and serve on a large dish, garnished with the sliced ginger pieces. A little wild and basmati rice is good with this.

Poussins stuffed with kumquats and pine nuts

Poussins are the small size chickens that are widely available now and which recently won a Good Housekeeping taste test for flavour. Though small they are also quite substantial and a whole one stuffed is probably more than a person can eat on their own. I find that half a poussin per person makes a wonderful main course in a dinner that has a starter and a dessert to go with it. Kumquats are a variety of tiny orange that you can eat whole.

INGREDIENTS
Serves 4

115 g/4 oz long grain or basmati rice

25 g/1 oz each olive oil and butter

55 g/2 oz pine nuts

1 tbsp orange marmalade

1 bunch of spring onions, white and green parts, finely chopped

Pinch of nutmeg

Salt and pepper

8 kumquats (tiny baby oranges)

2 poussins, oven-ready

1 Pre-heat the oven to 200°C/400°F/gas mark 6/middle of the roasting oven in the Aga.

2 Put the rice to boil in a pint of salted water. When it's barely cooked, about 8 to 9 minutes, drain thoroughly. Melt the butter in the oil and fry the pine nuts gently for about 2 to 3 minutes until they golden.

3 Add the marmalade and allow that to melt. Add the drained rice, the spring onions and the nutmeg, season generously and mix thoroughly together off the heat.

4 Cut the kumquats into quarters, remove any seeds that emerge, and mix the oranges with the rice.

5 Stuff the poussins carefully with the mixture, putting any extra stuffing into a baking dish. Season and roast them with the surplus stuffing, if any, in the baking dish alongside, for one hour. Check if the chickens are done by putting a skewer or sharp knife into the thigh. If they show any pink juices allow them to cook for another 10 minutes and check again.

6 To serve, split the poussins in half lengthways with a big, sharp knife, pile the stuffing onto warm plates and cover with the half poussins, skin side up. Beans are nice with this.

MUSIC RECOMMENDATION

It might seem a bit obvious considering the title of the dish but I think that Sergei Prokofiev's early opera *The Love for Three Oranges* would provide great incidental music to accompany this food. Perhaps the most famous bit is the 'comic' march which I remember seeing first at Sadler's Wells many years ago, being danced in the most exaggerated and hilarious style.

Chicken with crème fraîche

This is a lovely rich main course with enough lightness in it to be part of today's fashionable style of eating and enough substance to satisfy the hungriest guest. If you can get fresh tarragon which is available in many stores these days, so much the better, if not, freeze-dried tarragon will be the best for flavour. *Crème Fraîche* is France's equivalent to double cream and should be found next to it on your dairy counter. Serve the dish with rice or one of the small shaped and possibly coloured pastas. A simple vegetable like quick fried sliced courgettes goes best with it.

INGREDIENTS
Serves 4

1 tbsp each oil and butter

4 chicken breasts, boned or part boned

Juice of half a lemon

150 ml/5 fl oz Crème Fraîche

1 tbsp fresh tarragon or 1 tsp freeze dried

Salt and pepper

1 Heat the oil and butter together in a large solid frying pan. Put in the chicken breasts skin side down and allow to brown for 5 minutes. Turn over and cook for another 5 minutes.

2 Add a cup of water and the lemon juice, cover if possible, and allow to simmer gently for 15 minutes. The liquid should reduce to a thick syrup.

3 Remove the breasts to a warm serving dish or plate and add the cream and tarragon to the liquid left in the pan. Season, stir thoroughly, and bring to a brisk boil.

4 Simmer for 1 minute before pouring the sauce over the chicken breasts or spoon a little over and serve the rest in a sauceboat or jug.

Chicken with mango

South America, in a culinary sense, is one of the great unexplored areas of the world. This is a pity because it is not only a rich and varied continent, but also the source of so many of our regular food items from potatoes to chocolate. Surprising though it may seem, a mixture of fruit and meat is quite common, as is cream. South America is a huge producer of beef, and the obvious by-product, dairy produce, is much used in cooking, particularly in the southern cities. This recipe blends the succulence of chicken with the sharp sweetness of mango to make a really light and delicious combination.

INGREDIENTS
Serves 4

1 ripe mango

1 tbsp oil (not olive)

4 boneless chicken breasts or large thighs

150 ml/¼ pint double cream

1 tbsp chopped green coriander

Salt and pepper

1 Cut off the mango 'cheeks'. Peel these and cut the flesh into long thin strips. You should get 4–5 pieces from each cheek.

2 Melt the oil or butter in a medium frying pan and fry the chicken gently for 10 minutes on each side – keeping a lid on it will help to cook it more quickly.

3 Remove the chicken and turn the mango pieces in the juices until they are warmed through. Place the mango over the chicken.

4 Pour the cream into the pan and boil for 2 minutes, stir in the coriander and season with salt and pepper. Pour this carefully over the chicken and mango.

5 Serve with rice decorated with nasturtium or marigold flowers for a spectacular presentation.

Guinea fowl sauté with redcurrant sauce

Guinea fowl is a marvellous cross between poultry and game. It has a texture and flavour similar to chicken (and a bird will feed as many people as a medium-sized chicken) but it also has the richness characteristic of game dishes. It is widely available at about the same price as a good chicken. In this recipe, the richness of guinea fowl is brought out with an unusual sauce using redcurrant jelly, or you can use fresh redcurrants.

INGREDIENTS
Serves 4

1 tbsp sunflower oil

1 tbsp butter

4 guinea fowl portions (ask your butchery counter or use a big knife)

Salt and freshly ground black pepper

150 ml/¼ pint double cream or Greek yoghurt

2 tbsp redcurrant jelly or 55 g/2 oz fresh redcurrants and 1 tsp sugar

1 In a large frying pan heat the oil and butter. As soon as the sizzling stops add the guinea fowl portions, skin side down, and sauté for 5 minutes until golden. Turn them over and sauté for another 10–15 minutes over a low heat. You may wish to put the lid on to help them cook thoroughly.

2 When the guinea fowl is cooked through, season generously and pour the cream or yoghurt over the top. Stir so all the bits in the pan are absorbed into the sauce, and allow the cream to come briefly to the boil. DO NOT boil if you are using yoghurt or it may separate.

3 If you're using fresh redcurrants, take the stalks off and wash them, sprinkle with sugar, pour them into the pan and stir into the sauce. If you are using redcurrant jelly, stir it in until it melts into a wonderful swirly pink sauce.

4 Take the guinea fowl portions out of the pan, put them onto warmed plates and pour every last drop of sauce from the pan over the top of them!

5 Serve with mashed or new potatoes and butter-tossed green cabbage.

Spiced quails

This is the dish my father remembers eating after a day's hunting in the forests of his native Bengal. Then the birds that they ate were the ones that they'd shot during the day's hunting. Now however you can buy quails in supermarkets so it's not quite such hard work. They are very small birds and very delicate so the spicing needs to be as light-handed as it can. Though traditionally they were cooked over, and undoubtedly had the tang of, an open fire, a modern oven makes a good substitute. Half a bird makes a good first course, a quail each, eaten with a chapati or paratha bread (look next to the Indian sauces) and followed by a few other Indian vegetable dishes makes a feast.

INGREDIENTS
Serves 4

4 quails

4 tbsp butter

1/2 tsp each of ground coriander, ground cardamom and paprika

1/4 tsp each of ground bay leaves, chilli pepper and cinnamon

Juice of 1 lemon

1 Pre-heat the oven to 200°C/400°F/gas mark 6/top of the Aga roasting oven

2 Mash the spices with the butter until thoroughly blended. Spread a layer of this on the breasts and legs of the quail and put a tiny knob inside.

3 Squeeze the juice of a lemon over the quails and place them, packed fairly well together, on a rack in a baking tray, and put in the oven to cook. Leave them for 10 minutes then take them out and baste with the juices that will have fallen into the pan below the rack.

4 Move them apart a little and put back to roast for another 10 to 12 minutes. Before serving, pour the juices over them one last time. They are simple and subtly spiced and can, if you wish, be cut in half for small individual servings as part of a larger meal.

5 Serve with Indian bread and a raita salad – yoghurt with mint and grated cucumber.

Turkey scaloppini with lemon

For this dish buy the turkey breast fillets that are available on the poultry counter, or you may be able to buy ready-prepared scaloppini. The dish originated with veal, but for a variety of reasons few people cook veal at home now, and turkey makes a very acceptable substitute.

INGREDIENTS
Serves 4

350 g/12 oz fresh green and white tagliatelle

1 tbsp sunflower oil plus a little extra

450 g/1 lb turkey breast fillets

25 g/1 oz butter

1 tbsp chopped fresh sage or 1 tsp freeze-dried

125 ml/4 fl oz apple juice

Juice and grated rind of 1 lemon

225 ml/8 fl oz double cream

1 Put the tagliatelle into a pan of boiling salted water, add a drop of oil and cook for 5–6 minutes until just tender. Drain and toss in half of the butter. Arrange in a large oval serving dish and keep warm.

2 Cut the turkey breast fillets across the grain at an angle so that you have a number of mini steaks, about 5 cm/2 in x 4 cm/1½ in. If they are very thick you may want to flatten them slightly under a sheet of greaseproof with the back of a frying pan or a meat mallet. They should be about 5 mm/¼ in thick.

3 Put the oil and remaining butter into a large frying pan into which all the turkey will go in one turn. Heat it until the butter stops sizzling and add the scaloppini. Cook for 45 seconds to 1 minute, turn and cook for another 1–1½ minutes. They should be light gold on the outside but not cooked to a dryness.

4 Sprinkle over the sage, season generously and add the apple juice, scraping up the bits in the bottom of the pan. Put the scaloppini on top of the tagliatelle with a slotted spoon, arranging them neatly. Add the lemon juice, rind and double cream to the remaining liquid, stir thoroughly and bring to the boil, simmering for 2–3 minutes while the sauce amalgamates and goes pale gold. Pour over the scaloppini and serve immediately. Serve with a green salad.

MUSIC RECOMMENDATION

Any recipe with as Italian a name as Scaloppini must have something appropriate to accompany it. A bit of lush Italian opera comes to mind like Donizetti's *L'Elisir d'Amore*. However the dish is more delightful for its precision than its lushness so I'll opt for Bach's wonderful crisp keyboard concerto The Italian in F major, preferably played by Glen Gould.

Ginger duck breast with wild rice and asparagus

An exotic, modern style dish that's really for special occasions. Duck breast portions are readily available, but now you can be spoiled for choice. At the least you will probably find conventional Aylesbury duck and Barbary duck, a larger and leaner breed, and I've also seen Gressingham and Khaki…no really! The more unusual types tend to have a richer taste and to be bigger; so you may not want so many breasts and can slice down the finished product to share amongst diners.

INGREDIENTS
Serves 4

4 duck breasts, approximately 175 g/6 oz each

2 tsp freshly grated ginger or ginger purée from a jar

2 pieces of stem ginger in syrup plus 2 tbsp of the syrup

2 tbsp soy sauce

FOR THE WILD RICE:

55 g/2 oz butter

225 g/8 oz American easy cook long grain and wild rice mixture

4 cardamom pods, bruised

1 bunch of asparagus tips or fresh asparagus spears

Seasoning

1 In a heavy frying pan fry the duck breasts, skin side down, for 5 minutes over a medium heat and crisp the skin brown. Do not add any other oil. as the breasts themselves will produce a surprising amount of fat

2 Pour most of the fat out of the pan and discard. Turn the breasts over, add the ginger and 4–6 tbsp of water, turn the heat to moderate and cook for 12–15 minutes until the water has evaporated and the breasts are cooked through.

3 Slice the ginger from the syrup very thinly, add it and the syrup to the soy sauce and add to the pan with 3tbsp of water to create a small quantity of sauce. Leave to stand for 2 or 3 minutes off the heat. Remove the duck breasts and slice across with a very sharp knife into about 10 or 12 slices. Arrange these in a fan on each plate; add any meat juices to the sauce and pour over the slices.

4 To make the wild rice, while the duck is cooking, heat the butter in a medium-sized pan with a good lid. Add the rice and stir for 2–3 minutes. Add 600 ml/1 pint of water, the cardamom pods and a pinch of salt and bring to the boil. Turn down to a low simmer, cover and leave for 8 minutes.

5 Trim the asparagus so you only have the top end plus the spears and add to the pan, placing them on top of the rice, not stirring them in. Replace the lid and allow them to cook.

6 After the rice is fully cooked, another 5 to 7 minutes, the water should be completely absorbed and the asparagus tips bright green. Serve the pilau beside the sliced duck breasts with the asparagus tips on top.

Duck Montmorency (with cherries)

This method of roasting a duck is Chinese-derived and works like a dream. The recipe, however is French. Montmorency was a pre-Revolutionary French dukedom in the Southwest of France, famous for its cherries and, so legend has it, for a duke who insisted on having them with everything. As it happens, they go particularly well with duck. If you can, use the bittersweet cherries known as morellos, as their sharpness counteracts the sweetness of the duck perfectly.

INGREDIENTS
Serves 4

1 x 1.8 kg/4 lb oven-ready duck

2 tsp arrowroot blended with a little water

425 g/15 oz can morello cherries

Salt and freshly ground black pepper

1 Place the duck in a colander in the sink and pour over 600 ml/1 pint boiling water. Leave it to dry for 1–2 hours, then roast in a preheated oven, 200°C/400°F/gas mark 6/top of the Aga roasting oven, allowing 20 minutes per 450 g/1 lb. Put the duck on a rack over the roasting pan to let the fat drain.

2 When the duck is golden brown, remove from the pan and keep warm. Place 2 tablespoons of the pan drippings, the blended arrowroot and the cherries and their juice in a pan and bring to the boil until it thickens and clears. If you can't get bitter cherries or the syrup is very sweet, add the juice of a lemon to balance the sauce.

3 Season to taste and serve with the duck, accompanied by rice or creamed potatoes. A salad is good served afterwards.

DRINK RECOMMENDATION

A German works well. Try:

Ockfener Bockstein
Riesling 1997/98
Dr. Wagner – £5.55

MUSIC RECOMMENDATION

A taste of pre-revolutionary France should have something flamboyant and courtly and not too sentimental. I think some Rameau would do nicely. A leading composer at the royal court during part of the 18th century Rameau wrote countless pieces for court occasions, including many opera/ballets. *Les Indes Gallants* happens to be one of my favourites, and that of many Classic FM listeners.

Pheasant Forestière

A marvellous autumn dish. Buy them without any bacon or larding wrapping because we're going to cut them up and there's no point in adding saturated fat to some of the healthiest meat available. If you can find or buy wild mushrooms, do so. If not, a sort of halfway house are chestnut or oyster mushrooms. They have a richer taste that goes very well with the flavour of pheasant. A cock pheasant, though slightly tougher than a hen, will feed four people, the hen, by and large, only three.

INGREDIENTS
Serves 3–4

1 cleaned prepared pheasant

225 g/8 oz carrots

225 g/8 oz mushrooms

4 sticks celery

1 tbsp each oil and butter

1 large onion, chopped

10 pickling sized onions, peeled

4 tbsp red wine vinegar

300 ml/½ pint water

Bouquet garni (2 stalks celery, 1 bay leaf, 1 sprig thyme, 4 parsley stalks tied together with string)

2 tsp arrowroot or potato flour

1 Pre-heat the oven to 180°C/350°F/gas mark 4/bottom of the Aga roasting oven.

2 Joint the pheasant or get your butcher to joint it for you.

3 Cut the carrots into 5 cm/2 in long, 1 cm/½ in wide batons. Wash the mushrooms in boiling water and cut into walnut sized pieces if they are large. Trim the celery and slice it across the grain into 1 cm/½ in slices.

4 In an ovenproof casserole heat the butter in the oil and brown the pheasant pieces.

5 Add the chopped onion, celery and carrots and turn them in the juices. Pour in the wine vinegar, bring to the boil, and allow to almost boil away. Season generously with salt and pepper and add the water and the bouquet garni. Bring back to the boil, cover and simmer for 25 minutes. Add the mushrooms and pickling onions and place in the oven for 20 minutes.

6 Mix the arrowroot or potato flour (or cornflour at a pinch) into a little water to make a smooth paste and stir it into the casserole. Heat through until at boiling point when the sauce will thicken and clear. Serve sprinkled with parsley, making sure each person gets a portion of baby onions and mushrooms and carrots as well as pheasant.

7 Potatoes in some form are essential with this, boiled and buttered, mashed or new, and that's not just an Irish opinion.

MUSIC RECOMMENDATION

Though Vivaldi is the composer one thinks of when the seasons are mentioned, be a little more adventurous and try Joseph Haydn's work *Autumn*. Written close to the end of his long life, it was supposed to have been inspired by hearing Handel's *Messiah* in Westminster Abbey. Haydn's *Autumn* is different from Vivaldi's but it is as moving.

Venison sausages with lentils

If you cannot find venison sausages, ask! They are worth it and they should not be difficult to get hold of. If there is a problem, try to buy good quality coarse ground beef sausages instead. Traditionally, this dish is cooked with the lentils and the sausages kept separate until they arrive on the plate. I think that putting them together for a little while beforehand improves the flavour and texture of both.

INGREDIENTS
Serves 4

225 g/8 oz green or brown lentils (the red ones won't do for this)

2 tbsp olive oil

225 g/8 oz onions, chopped

4 stalks of celery, diced

2 carrots, diced

4 plum or similar tomatoes

700 g/1 lb 8 oz venison sausages

1 tsp fennel seeds (optional)

Salt and pepper

DRINK RECOMMENDATION

A hearty southern Rhône works well.

Gigondas 1996/97
Domaine Sainte Lucie –
£8.99

1 Soak the lentils in plenty of water for at least 1 hour and up to 6 hours. Throw the water away.

2 Into a pan which will take all the lentil ingredients and the sausages in due course, put the olive oil and gently fry the onion, celery, and carrot. Add the lentils. Cover with water to a depth of 2.5 cm/1 in above and bring to the boil.

3 Simmer gently for about half an hour until the lentils are cooked and almost all the water is absorbed. You may need to add a little more water depending on the individual lentils you're using. Chop up the tomatoes and add those to the lentil mixture, seasoning generously at this point.

4 Fry the sausages, either in their own fat or in a little extra oil, until they are well browned. Add them and the fennel seeds, if you are using them, to the lentil mixture, making sure that the mixture is still quite runny and moist. Cook with the lid on and the sausages at least partly buried for another 15 minutes over a very low heat for the flavours to blend.

5 Serve each person their sausages and lentils in a deep plate. The lentils should still be, while not soupy, quite moist and runny. No other vegetable is needed at this point. A good salad afterwards is very refreshing.

Rabbit with rosemary and marjoram

Rabbit is a very popular meat in Italy where this recipe originated – far more so than in Britain where it tends to be regarded as a poor relation. This method of cooking with very little liquid is used for a lot of game including pigeon, guinea fowl and, occasionally, pheasant. This dish used to be cooked in a parchment case but you can use foil now, though I prefer doing it in a saucepan with a really close fitting lid. A layer of foil under the lid is probably a satisfactory way of achieving the seal if your lids are a bit loose.

INGREDIENTS
Serves 4

3 tbsp olive oil

1 rabbit, jointed, ask at the butcher's counter.

1 clove of garlic

1 sprig of fresh rosemary

2 sprigs of fresh oregano or marjoram

2 bayleaves

Juice and grated rind of 1 lemon

1 Heat the oil in the bottom of a saucepan into which the pieces will all just fit and sauté the rabbit for 2–3 minutes until sealed on the outside. Crush the garlic but do not remove from its wrapper. Add that and place the herbs amongst the rabbit pieces. Dried herbs do not work as well, as they will stick to the pieces of rabbit and change the intended flavour.

2 Pour over the juice of the lemon and add the grated rind. Shake gently to mix everything together. Put on an airtight lid and cook over the lowest possible heat. A heat-diffusing pad is often useful in this connection.

3 The rabbit should be cooked through in about 40 minutes and should have a very little, but intensely flavoured, juice at the bottom of the pan. Season it generously with salt and pepper before serving.

I think it goes well with tagliatelle, well coated with butter. Any vegetables should be a separate course.

DRINK RECOMMENDATION

Soft Spanish reds are delicious with rabbit.
Viña Fuerte Garnacha 1998 Calatayud Spain – £3.99

Fish

Of all the dishes broadcast on Classic FM, Henry Kelly's favourite was a little unexpected. Now the unexpected is what you come to expect from Henry, him being Irish and all, and in this case it was a dish of cod and peppers, something with strong Spanish overtones, though the Spanish might make it with their beloved hake rather than cod. It's a very pretty dish with the glistening white fish nestling on top of a colourful bed of mixed peppers, but what the choice shows is how far fish has been rehabilitated in the last few years.

Ten years ago it was all doom and gloom, with sales of fish falling dramatically and even 'fish and chippers' being replaced by doner kebabs as fast food outlets. The trends towards healthier eating, a better presentation of fish products, fashion and Harry Ramsdens' have all done their part to put fish back on the menu again. Most new supermarkets have a fish counter and it's really worth asking advice and getting the hard work like filleting or skinning done for you by the experts who service them. I've included a number of recipes for different kinds of fish as the variety the different species offer is a great part of their attraction. What they all share is ease of preparation and the absence of the dubious smells that I can recall from my own childhood. This is definitely fish for the 21st century.

Spanish cod with peppers

If this dish has a subtitle it is 'Henry Kelly's Favourite'. There was a time when he seemed to be eating it almost weekly. I think it is the eye appeal of the dish as well as the clear and succulent tastes that make it so popular. Much modern food preparation now has plainly cooked fish just placed on top of some garnish or another. It may be fashionable, but to me it often looks a bit brutal and tastes arbitrary; this dish on the other hand, though the fish is beautifully and cleanly presented, both looks and tastes integrated … just like Henry.

INGREDIENTS
Serves 4

2 red and 2 green peppers

3 tbsp olive oil

1 spanish onion

1 large beef or marmande tomato

Salt and pepper

4 x 175 g/6 oz cod steaks, trimmed

1 tbsp chopped parsley

1 Trim the peppers, remove the seeds and slice them into thin strips about 5 mm/¼ in wide. Fry these gently in the oil in a frying pan with a lid, while peeling and slicing the onion similarly. Add the onion and cook for 10 minutes on a low heat without browning, stirring occasionally.

2 Slice the tomato across the grain into 4 slices, arrange these on the peppers and put a piece of fish on each tomato slice. Season (white pepper looks best) and put on the lid and cook for another 8 minutes until the fish is cooked through and a brilliant white. Do NOT turn the fish or spoon the sauce over.

3 Sprinkle with the parsley and serve direct from the pan using a fish slice, to preserve the look of each portion. Some new potatoes or plain rice are a good balance.

MUSIC RECOMMENDATION

I remember Henry playing a piece of Rodrigo's guitar music to go with this recipe and very appropriate it was too, but I can't for the life of me remember which bit it was. Rodrigo, who was blind from childhood, is probably the greatest guitar composer this century, so let's choose his most famous piece, the nostalgic *Concierto de Aranjuez* or as it was memorably described in the film Brassed Off, Concerto de Orange Juice.

Herb stuffed trout

I have chosen to use trout in this recipe, as it is a great fishy bargain! It isn't expensive, you can buy it cleaned and ready to cook and the bones are easy to handle. This recipe looks and sounds grand and impressive but it really is very simple to prepare. If you can find unwaxed or organic lemons, use them. Dill is the feathery bright green herb that goes so well with fish.

INGREDIENTS
Serves 4

70 g/2½ oz softened butter

4 trout about
175–225 g/6 oz–8 oz each

175 g/6 oz white breadcrumbs

1 egg, beaten

1–2 tbsp chopped fresh parsley

1 tbsp chopped fresh dill or 2 tsp freeze dried dill

2 spring onions, trimmed and finely chopped

Salt and freshly ground black pepper

Grated rind and juice of 1 lemon

1 Pre-heat the oven to 200°C/400°F/gas mark 6/top of the Aga roasting oven

2 Cut four large pieces from a roll of silver foil or cooking parchment so each is big enough to wrap a trout loosely. Butter one side of each piece thoroughly. Put a cleaned and trimmed fish into the middle of each square, across the diagonal.

3 In a mixing bowl, mix the breadcrumbs, beaten egg, chopped parsley, dill, spring onions, salt, pepper and softened butter. Mix until it is really smooth. Add the grated lemon peel and half the juice, mix again and stuff the cavity of each trout with the mixture, pressing in well.

4 Pour the remaining lemon juice over the fish, season again, and fold the foil or parchment over the trout to make a loose parcel. Make sure the edges are closely folded to keep in all the steam and juices.

5 Place on a baking tray and cook for 20–25 minutes.

6 To serve, put the unopened packets – support each with a fish slice – onto warmed plates and allow each person to open the packet themselves and be engulfed in the wonderful herby, lemony, buttery steam! Serve with new potatoes and little green beans.

MUSIC RECOMMENDATION

I know it's obvious but I don't care. Franz Schubert's exquisite Piano Quintet known as *The Trout* is one of my favourite pieces of music, capturing all the lightness and grace of this quicksilver fish. The recipe is a bit of a favourite too; so … what better than to put together two pleasures at once. The piece is just long enough to match to a meal.

Moules Normande

Mussels are the cheapest of shellfish and are very widely available. You can now buy them fresh and ready cleaned and that saves a lot of hard work. You still need to check the cleaned ones thoroughly, though. Put them into a bowl of clean water. Remove any beards that are still attached by pulling gently. Check to make sure there are no cracked shells. If any are open or loose, give them a slight tap. Unless they close at once, throw them away. It is not worth taking any risk. This way of cooking them is the Normandy version of making *Moules Marinière*. They use their beloved apple products, in the form of juice or cider rather than water or wine.

INGREDIENTS
Serves 4

1 kg/2 lb 4 oz cleaned mussels

1 clove garlic, chopped

175 ml/6 fl oz apple juice

Salt and pepper

150 ml/¼ pint double cream

1 tsp cornflour

2 tbsp chopped parsley

1 Put the cleaned mussels, garlic and apple juice into a large saucepan and season. Bring to the boil; cover with a lid and cook at maximum heat for 5 minutes, shaking the pan frequently. The mussels will open when cooked.

2 Take them off the heat and throw away any mussels that have not opened. Put the rest in a bowl. Sprinkle with a little salt and pepper.

3 Mix together the cream and cornflour until you have a smooth paste. Add this to the liquid in the saucepan (there should be about a cup; if not add a little more juice or water) and stir. Bring back to the boil, and spoon this lovely slightly sweet, creamy sauce over the cooked mussels.

4 Sprinkle the parsley over and have lots of crusty bread to mop up the juices.

DRINK RECOMMENDATION

A Muscadet is ideal
Waitrose Muscadet de
Sèvre et Maine 'Sur Lie'
1998 – £4.49

Sweet and sour prawns

We tend to think of sweet and sour sauce as a kind of red and glutinous Chinese tomato ketchup. And to add insult to injury, much of the sweet and sour sauce served in Chinese takeaway restaurants is heavily dosed with monosodium glutamate. Made properly in China, the sauce's colour varies from region to region, and at its best is subtle and spicy. This version comes from the northern part of China and is brown, not red, to set off the prawns. Serve it with rice and stir-fried bean sprouts.

INGREDIENTS
Serves 4

1½ tbsp cornflour

100 ml/3½ fl oz orange juice

100 ml/3 1/2 fl oz soya sauce

1 tbsp brown sugar

2 tbsp cider vinegar

½ tsp garlic salt

½ tsp ground ginger

1 tbsp oil

1 tbsp tomato purée (optional)

2 tbsp crushed pineapple (optional)

450 g/1 lb large cooked peeled prawns (tiger prawns are best for this)

1 Mix the cornflour with the orange juice until smooth. Mix with all the other ingredients except the prawns and bring to the boil in a saucepan, stirring regularly until thick and smooth. (Optional additions are 1 tablespoon of tomato purée if you want a red sauce, 2 tablespoons of crushed pineapple, or both.)

2 Add the prawns and heat for 1 more minute only before serving. If you want to make this dish with raw prawns, fry them in a little oil till they turn pink and then add the sauce ingredients and cook for not more than 3 minutes. In both cases the prawns will shrivel if overcooked.

DRINK RECOMMENDATION

The natural home for any good German Riesling Spatelese style, preferably young.
'Dr. L' Riesling 1997/98 Dr. Loosen – £5.99

Rich fish pie

This is a great favourite. I always make double the quantity I think I need and watch it disappear! What makes it so good is the mixture of fresh and smoked fish, which gives it extra texture and flavour. If you can find it, use undyed smoked fish.

INGREDIENTS
Serves 4

700 g/1 lb 9 oz mashing potatoes

450 g/1 lb cod or any firm white fish – skinned and boned

450 g/1 lb smoked haddock or smoked cod-skinned and boned

300 ml/½ pint full cream milk

225 g/8 oz button mushrooms

70 g/2½ oz butter

40 g/1½ oz plain flour

A good pinch of grated nutmeg

2 small onions or half a Spanish onion, peeled and finely chopped

Salt and pepper

4 hard boiled eggs

1 Pre-heat the oven to 180°C/350°F/gas mark 4/bottom of the Aga roasting oven

2 Peel the potatoes, cut into chunks and boil for 10–15 minutes in plenty of salted water until soft enough to mash. Put all the boned and skinned fish into another saucepan, pour in the milk and poach gently for a couple of minutes only. Do not cook it fully just yet. Scald the mushrooms in boiling water to clean them, then cut into quarters.

3 Take the fish out of the milk (which you leave in the saucepan) and flake it into chunks and leave to one side.

4 To make a white sauce, whisk the flour and 40 g/1½ oz of the butter into the milk. Add the pinch of nutmeg, season if necessary and whisk over the heat until it becomes a thick, glossy sauce as it boils.

5 Mix the mushrooms and flaked fish into the sauce, then pour into a pie dish. Spread a layer of onion on top. Halve the eggs and place them on the onion, cut side up. Drain and mash the cooked potatoes with the remaining butter, season and then, spoonful by spoonful, cover the top of the onion and fish until all the potato is on top of the pie, then smooth the top gently with a fork.

6 Bake for about 25–30 minutes until the top is just starting to go crispy brown and the sauce is bubbling underneath. The layers of flavour in this are just delicious.

DRINK RECOMMENDATION

Remarkably, a cup of Earl Grey tea is hard to beat! Otherwise, any light, crisp dry white.

Baked snapper

Snapper is a favourite fish of people who live in the Tropics. It's a fish which benefits from baking whole. It's quite difficult to fillet when raw but when cooked the very solid flesh lifts easily off the bones. This is for a 1–1.5 kg/2–3 lb fish, which will easily feed four people. Snappers are widely available in Britain now, but you could also use Tilapia fish as well.

INGREDIENTS
Serves 4

1 large snapper or Tilapia 1–1.5 kg/2–3 lb cleaned

1 tsp salt

4 tbsp oil

1 red chilli pepper (finely shredded)

2 limes

1 faggot (small bunch) of herbs made up of thyme, spring onion, bay leaf and celery leaf

1 Pre-heat the oven to180°C/350°F/gas mark 4/bottom of the Aga roasting oven

2 Wash the fish inside and out and rub with a little salt.

3 Take a piece of foil large enough to wrap around the fish loosely and use half the oil to grease it. Mix the rest of the oil with the chopped chilli and slice one of the limes thinly. Put a line of lime slices down the foil, place the fish on top, and spread the chilli and oil mixture on this side only.

4 Lay the remaining lime slices on top of the fish. Stuff the cavity with the herbs. Squeeze the other lime over the fish and fold the foil together loosely to form an airtight package without clamping it down on the fish. Bake for 55 to 60 minutes until the fish is cooked right through.

5 Try and serve the fish whole to the table, as it looks splendid. Serve each person a portion of fish and a spoonful of the juices. I serve this with crusty bread, but rice is also nice.

DRINK RECOMMENDATION

Quite a meaty, oily fish. Try a fruity soft red.

Don Hugo, Vino de Mesa, Spain – £3.95

Creamed smoked haddock

If you're eating alone why not treat yourself with this delicious, comforting supper dish which can be varied by adding assorted toppings. My favourite is a soft poached egg, which blends into the flavours and textures of the haddock perfectly. To make this go further and to serve two people, you could put it into a dish, surround it with mashed potato, and just flash it under the grill to crisp the top. Or for a substantial starter, individual portions are great with a little cheese on top before you brown them. Make lots… there's never enough. If cooking for up to four, increase the fish and onion but not the liquids.

INGREDIENTS
Serves 1–2

175 g/6 oz smoked haddock fillet

300 ml/¹/₂ pint milk

300 ml/¹/₂ pint water

¹/₂ sweet onion

2 tsp cornflour

15 g/¹/₂ oz butter

1 Put the haddock with the milk and water into a pan, bring it to the boil and poach for 5 minutes. Peel the half onion and chop very finely, adding it to the haddock and milk as they come to the boil.

2 Take the haddock out of the liquid and skin. Roughly flake the flesh.

3 To a 300 ml/¹/₂ pint of the milk mixture add the cornflour and butter, and whisk over a gentle heat until the sauce thickens. Put the haddock back into the sauce and heat through. You can serve this with mashed potatoes or my favourite, granary toast.

DRINK RECOMMENDATION

A soft, ripe French sauvignon works quite well.

Waitrose Bordeaux Sauvignon 1998 – £3.69

Fish cakes

These are quite unlike any fish cakes you have ever eaten, or at least I hope they are. I have recently seen signs of others catching on to the delicious possibilities of a mixture of fresh and smoked fish. If by the way, you think fishcakes are only for breakfast, serve these in the evening with some green beans and a rich tomato sauce to learn the error of your ways.

INGREDIENTS
Serves 4

225 g/8 oz cod

225 g/8 oz smoked cod or haddock

300 ml/½ pint milk

½ tsp nutmeg

450 g/1 lb potatoes, boiled

25 g/1 oz butter

1 egg, beaten

2 heaped tbsp soft breadcrumbs

1–2 tbsp vegetable oil

1 Put the fish, milk and a pinch of nutmeg into a saucepan, bring to the boil, cover and simmer very gently for about 10 minutes. Drain, skin and flake the fish into quite small pieces, making sure you remove any bones. Keep the milk.

2 Mash the boiled potatoes with ½ teaspoon nutmeg, the butter and a spoonful of the reserved milk to make a dry smooth mash – not a gloppy one! Add the fish and mix thoroughly into the potatoes.

3 Divide into 8 balls, then flatten slightly into cakes. Allow to cool, then dip first into the beaten egg, then into the breadcrumbs, pressing them in firmly until each cake is well coated. Chill for at least 1 hour before frying. Fry them in a tablespoon or two of oil for 5–7 minutes on each side until a rich, golden brown.

Meat

The fashion for large joints or even big pieces of meat seems to have quite gone from our kitchens. This was not the case in the past. It was not for nothing that the British were, and still are, known to the French as les Rosbifs. (Isn't it funny how we all use food as an insult, with our 'frogs' and 'krauts' for the French and Germans?) We used to have a taste for meat in large quantities, but all the usual factors from health to vegetarianism have eroded this. I suspect, at least on Sundays at lunchtime, the old habit remains, if most pub menus and their crowded tables are anything to go by.

But it is a fact that we are eating less red meat and happily paying more attention to where it comes from and how it is reared. We are also using meat more for the intensity of taste it brings rather than as a bulk ingredient. It is that trend I have tried to highlight in some of these recipes chosen from the many meat dishes we broadcast. There are some traditional casseroles and braises, but also some lighter ideas like the pitta pizzas and a couple of exotic eastern flavours that proved so popular with our listeners. Meat is, these days, safer than ever before, and adds, unless you have given it up altogether, so much to savour to our meals that I am glad to be part of the movement to rehabilitate its rather battered image.

Carbonade of beef

In Europe every country cooks its beef in whatever liquid, water, juice, cider, wine or beer it has handy. This recipe from Belgium uses lager to make a lovely rich gravy. The name of the dish by the way is supposed to refer to the taste for it, developed by the hearty appetites of the South Belgian coal miners, the name for coal being charbon.

INGREDIENTS
Serves 6

900 g/2 lb stewing beef

55 g/2 oz flour

1 tbsp vegetable oil

25 g/1 oz butter

450 g/1 lb onions, sliced

1 large clove garlic, chopped

300 ml/¹/₂ pint lager

300 ml/¹/₂ pint beef stock

Bouquet garni (bought ready prepared) or made out of celery, parsley stalks, thyme and a bay leaf tied together with string.

¹/₂ tsp dried thyme

2 tbsp chopped parsley to garnish

Salt and freshly ground black pepper

1 Pre-heat the oven to 170°C/325°F/gas mark 3/Aga simmering oven.

2 Cut the meat into small pieces, 5 mm/¹/₄ in thick. Dust with some of the flour. Heat the oil and butter together in a frying pan and fry the meat for about 5 minutes until brown. Transfer to a casserole.

3 Fry the onions in the same oil for 2 minutes, add the garlic and cook for 1 minute more.

4 Sprinkle with the remaining flour, then mix with the beef. Rinse out the hot frying pan with the lager and add to the beef with the stock. Season to taste with salt and pepper, add the bouquet garni and thyme and cook in a preheated oven for 1¹/₂ hours. Remove the bouquet garni.

5 Sprinkle with the parsley and serve with mashed potatoes. Any vegetables should be served as a course on their own.

DRINK RECOMMENDATION

Remarkably tricky to match due to the beer. A rich, mellow Australian Shiraz would be safest.

Peter Lehmann Shiraz 1997 Barossa Valley – £6.99

Pitta bread pizzas

Coming from the Middle East, pitta bread has become common place in our high streets, in every doner kebab shop. Pitta is so easy to use at home but this delicious light meal is a very dangerous recipe. I've never been able to make enough. If your grill can take three or four slices of pitta, a family party can devour them and regain its appetite by the time the next batch is ready. Beware, and make plenty! These work well on a barbecue, particularly if your barbecue has a lid.

INGREDIENTS
Serves 4 (maybe)

3 pitta bread, sliced open into 6 flat pieces

325 g/12 oz minced beef

1 medium onion, very finely chopped

1 tbsp tomato purée

2 tbsp freshly chopped coriander or parsley

1 tsp allspice

1 tsp cinnamon

A little oil

Salt and pepper

Parsley or coriander leaves to decorate

1 Carefully cut the pitta open to make 6 bases for 'open' sandwiches. You may want to warm it to help with this. Place the pitta under the grill 'crumb' side up and lightly toast to stop it going soggy when filled. If using a barbecue place crumb side down for 1 minute.

2 Mix all the other ingredients together and spread a thin layer of mince onto the cut side of the pitta, covering the entire surface. Grill for 5 minutes and serve. If cooking on a barbecue place the pitta on foil or a strong baking tray to prevent burning and use a barbecue lid.

3 You can decorate the pitta with some chopped parsley or coriander leaves. Though it's not refined, the best way to eat these is with your fingers.

Lamb tagine

A Moroccan version of a lamb and fruit stew that's popular all along the North African coast and the Middle East. Use neck, best end of neck or middle neck chops, they are cheaper and have bags of flavour. It is advisable to order these cuts in advance from your butcher. If using neck, ask him to cut it into 2.5 cm/1 in rounds. For the lentils, you can use red or yellow lentils, or the slightly larger yellow *Chana dal*, available where you get dried pulses, or from an Indian specialist.

INGREDIENTS
Serves 4–6

2 tbsp olive oil

750 g–1 kg/
1 lb 10 oz–2 lb 4 oz lamb
(as above)

450 g/1 lb onions, chopped

1 clove of garlic, chopped

55 g/2 oz red or yellow lentils

1 tsp ginger

1 tsp coriander

½ tsp cinnamon

A pinch of salt

115 g/4 oz dried apricots

2 tbsp browned, slivered almonds

1 Heat the oil in a large flameproof casserole, and brown the lamb. Add the onions, garlic and lentils and stir. Add the spices and salt and cook for 1 minute before adding enough water to just cover the lamb pieces.

2 Add the apricots, cover the pan and cook for 1 hour on a low heat. The lentils and apricots will absorb the water and thicken the stew.

3 Serve with spinach, on a bed of pilau rice or cous cous, and sprinkle with the almonds just before serving.

Spring lamb stew

We don't enjoy seasonal food as much as we used to. Spring and in particular spring lamb is a rare exception to this. Tender lamb does not need hours of cooking, so as well as being delicious, the dish is also quite quick to make. It is a marvellous combination of juicy lamb and crisp vegetables. The trick is to add the vegetables when the meat is nearly done, so the whole lot is just cooked at the same moment.

INGREDIENTS
Serves 4

750 g/1 lb 10 oz boneless fillet of lamb, cut into 5 cm x 1 cm/2 x ½ in pieces

2 tbsp flour

1 tbsp vegetable oil

225 g/8 oz onions, peeled and sliced

600 ml/1 pint lamb or beef stock or water

225 g/8 oz each new carrots and turnips, scrubbed and cut into batons

225 g/8 oz green beans topped and tailed

1 tsp salt

225 g/8 oz button mushrooms

15 g/½ oz butter

1 tbsp tomato purée

Pinch each freeze-dried or a sprig each of fresh thyme and marjoram

Freshly ground black pepper

1 Toss the lamb pieces in the flour until well coated. The easiest way to do this is in a large paper or plastic bag. Heat the oil in a large pan and fry the lamb for 10 minutes, turning occasionally so it browns all over. Add the sliced onions and stock, bring to the boil, and then simmer for 10 minutes. Add the carrot and turnip batons and beans, the herbs and seasonings, then cover the pan and simmer for another 10 minutes.

2 Clean the mushrooms by putting them into a colander and pouring a kettle of boiling water over them. Don't peel them. Heat the butter in a saucepan and when it has melted, toss the mushrooms quickly in the butter until well coated.

3 Add the mushrooms to the lamb; add the tomato purée and heat through for 1 minute, stirring so the tomato purée is absorbed into the sauce.

4 Serve with new potatoes in their skins and a salad to follow.

MUSIC RECOMMENDATION

No, not Vivaldi or even Johann Strauss' II's *Voices of Spring*, but to go with this bright dish a, for me recently discovered, treasure. The young Schumann's *Symphony No.1*, subtitled *Spring*. I find much of the later Schumann work heavy, and introspective. But this early piece is lively and full of cheerful tunes that justify its title admirably.

Crafty cassoulet

This dish is adapted from one of the national dishes of France – *Cassoulet*. Essentially it's a bean bake – a dish of dried beans soaked, cooked till almost tender and then flavoured and enriched. As you would expect with the French, when they enrich, they enrich! – preserved goose, pieces of roast lamb, special sausages and so on. But a very acceptable – indeed delicious – version can be made simply. When you buy the beans don't buy the big type of butter beans. Good haricot beans are round and kidney-shaped and often quite small – when they are dry. They expand remarkably when they are soaked. (It's traditional to use white beans for this, but kidney beans in all colours, red, green, black and spotted, are equally as good. If you are using dried red kidney beans boil them thoroughly for at least 15 minutes.) As for the sausages, I prefer beef or the lamb *merguez* sausages that seem to be creeping onto the market. Sausages with some texture are certainly nicer. Don't use frankfurters.

INGREDIENTS
Serves 4

325 g/12 oz dried haricot beans

325 g/12 oz coarse cut beef sausages

1 onion peeled and thinly sliced

1 clove of garlic peeled and chopped

2 tbsp oil

1 tbsp tomato purée

Salt and pepper

1/2 tsp each of dried thyme and marjoram

115 g/4 oz breadcrumbs

1 Soak the beans in a large saucepan of fresh water for at least 4–6 hours. Change the water, and cover the beans with at least 5 cm/2 in. Bring to the boil and boil for 10 minutes. Change the water and then simmer for 1½ hours.

2 Pre-heat the oven to 180°C/350°F/gas mark 4/top of the Aga simmering oven.

3 Fry the sausages, onion and garlic in the oil until brown. Stir the tomato purée into the cooked beans, which should have absorbed the water but still be moist. Add the sausage mixture, stirring gently. Season generously, adding the herbs to taste. Cover with the breadcrumbs and bake for 30 minutes to an hour.

4 Serve in soup plates. It needs nothing but a pud to follow.

DRINK RECOMMENDATION

A young, firm, spicy red
Chianti Classico 1996/97
Rocca di Castagnoli –
£7.49

Stir fry beef and basil

This is one of the basic dishes of Thai cooking, adapted for easily accessible ingredients. It is delicious eaten with rice and a stir-fried vegetable dish. In Thailand it would be part of a much larger group of dishes eaten as part of a selection on the buffet table, and you can, if you like, try it that way as well, with other Chinese or Thai style dishes included. It's very simple to cook and also very quick, so it makes for a really fresh convenience dish, with a high flavour impact.

INGREDIENTS
Serves 4

1 tbsp cooking oil (not olive)

450 g/1 lb lean minced beef or steak

2 tbsp soy sauce, or Thai fish sauce

1 tsp each garlic and ginger paste

½ tsp chilli paste or sauce

12 fresh basil leaves

Grated rind and juice of 1 fresh lime

1 Heat the oil in a heavyweight frying pan and brown the meat in it thoroughly.

2 Add the soy sauce or, more authentically, fish sauce, and the garlic, ginger and chilli and turn over a low heat until the flavours are blended and the mixture is almost dry.

3 Shred the basil leaves and add those and the lime peel and mix together thoroughly and then sprinkle with the lime juice.

4 Check for seasoning and serve with plenty of boiled rice and a stir-fried vegetable.

DRINK RECOMMENDATION

Thai 'Singha' beer, or an off-dry German Riesling

Devonshire lamb pie

This is a modern version of a really ancient style of pie, the kind from which our mince pies, which we eat as sweet food at Christmas, derived. It comes from the mediaeval period, a time when spices and dried fruit were used to eke out sparse amounts of often less than well-preserved meat in wintertime. I like this recipe because I think that lamb or mutton already has an inherent sweetness in it, which the seasoning and other ingredients bring out.

INGREDIENTS
Serves 4

900 g/2 lb stewing lamb (preferably boned)

1 large onion, chopped

2 eating apples

1 tbsp all spice

½ tbsp nutmeg

1 tbsp brown sugar (soft brown, not demerara)

12 prunes, stoned

300 ml/½ pint stock or water (chicken cube stock will do)

450 g/1 lb shortcrust pastry

1 egg, beaten

1 Pre-heat the oven to 180°C/350°F/gas mark 4/bottom of the Aga roasting oven.

2 Cut the meat into small pieces, about the size of a walnut half, then fry gently in their own fat in a saucepan. Add the onion.

3 Core the apples and cut them into segments. I use an apple corer to do this, a really useful gadget that produces 12 even-sized pieces.

4 When the meat has thoroughly browned, put half into a pie dish, cover with half the apple pieces, sprinkle with the sugar and spices, and add half the prunes.

5 Repeat the process with lamb, prunes next this time and then apple on the top. Pour in enough stock or water to come just below the top layer of apples. The prunes will absorb a lot of this as it cooks so don't worry if it looks too liquid.

6 Cut a strip of pastry and put it onto the wetted edge of the pie dish. Roll out the remaining pastry, cover the pie, crimp, trim, decorate, and brush with beaten egg. Bake for an hour and a quarter to an hour and a half. You may need to cover the pastry towards the end of the cooking with a piece of greaseproof paper to stop it browning too fast.

7 Eat it hot with some boiled potatoes and some carrots and sprouts for colour.

Texas barbecued lamb

Although Texas is rather more famous for its beef than its lamb there has always been a tradition, particularly in those parts of the huge state where beef cattle don't flourish, for growing lamb. Indeed, at the end of the 19th century, the most vicious range wars were fought between sheep and cattle farmers for the use of grazing and water. There's no violence involved in this dish however, just the slightly spicy sour and sweet flavours that are associated with the outdoor cooking of this part of America that's next to Mexico.

INGREDIENTS
Serves 4

900 g/2 lb boneless lamb, fillet, shoulder or leg, cut into 2.5 cm/1 in cubes

1 large onion

1 clove of garlic

50 ml/2 fl oz oil (not olive)

1 tsp each dried thyme, sage and powdered cumin

1/2 tsp mustard powder

1/2 tsp cayenne pepper

1 tsp salt

1 tbsp soft brown sugar

1 tbsp cider vinegar

500 ml/18 fl oz passata (sieved Italian tomato purée)

1 Peel and finely chop the onion and the garlic and cook gently in a non-stick pan in the oil until translucent but not brown. Add the spices and herbs and stir for a minute or two. Add the vinegar, sugar and passata.

2 Stir and simmer gently for 5 minutes and then partially cover and simmer at the lowest possible heat for another 15 minutes, making sure that the mixture doesn't burn or stick.

3 Allow to cool then marinate the lamb cubes in this barbecue mixture for at least an hour and up to 24 hours.

4 Thread close together onto 8 skewers and grill over a high heat or under a pre-heated grill for 4 to 5 minutes, turning to grill for another 3 or 4 minutes and then turning one last time for a last 3 to 4 minutes. The lamb should be crisp on the outside but still succulent on the inside.

5 Meanwhile, reheat the marinade, bring it to the boil again, and allow to simmer for 5 minutes.

6 Serve with the barbecued lamb skewers. Rice or soft flour tortillas (Mexican bread) are best with this.

Lamb korma

Kormas are one of the great triumphs of Mogul cookery, the style of food that developed in the Indian Emperors' courts in the 16th and 17th centuries. Famed for their luxury and wealth, they had a great taste for good food and Northern Indian cooking reached its peak under their rule. This dish is neither hot nor sharp, but creamy, rich and positively sumptuous. It's best eaten with plainly boiled long grain rice, a vegetable dish like lemon spinach or cauliflower and peas, and a raita salad made from yoghurt and finely chopped tomatoes, cucumbers and mint.

INGREDIENTS
Serves 4

2 tbsp oil or ghee (clarified or cooking butter)

2 tsp each ground garlic and ginger paste (or grind 2 cloves of garlic with a 2.5 cm/1 in piece of peeled fresh ginger)

450 g/1 lb thinly sliced onions

2 tsp ground coriander

1 tsp each of ground cardamom and ground cumin seed

900 g/2 lb boned leg of lamb or lamb fillet

175 ml/6 fl oz Greek style yoghurt

1/2 tsp each of cloves and ground bay leaves and cinnamon

55 g/2 oz ground almonds

1 Put the oil or ghee in a large thick saucepan and heat it. Add the ginger and garlic and the onions and fry gently for 10–15 minutes until the onions are pale gold and completely soft. Add all the spices except the cloves, cinnamon and bay leaves, and cook gently with the onion for 4 minutes.

2 Cut the lamb into 2.5 cm/1 in cubes, add that and turn until thoroughly coated with the onion and spice mixture. Add a cup of water and the yoghurt, which you should stir before adding so that it is completely smooth. Season generously.

3 Bring the mixture to the boil and turn down to the lowest possible simmer, covering with a close fitting lid. Cook for 30–40 minutes until the lamb is tender.

4 Mix the ground almonds with a little milk and stir them into the sauce with the remaining spices. Simmer gently for 5 minutes until thickened and serve with boiled rice and vegetable accompaniments. You can add a pinch of sugar and a squeeze of lemon juice to the sauce before serving.

MUSIC RECOMMENDATION

As this was a dish developed for an emperor, a piece of music which evokes imperial themes would be appropriate, Not British imperial dreams like Elgar, but Viennese Imperial tastes with Beethoven's *Emperor* piano concerto No 5. Haydn, who taught Beethoven, used to call him the Grand Mogul because of his difficulties of temperament.

Bhuna Ghosht (meat curry)

This, like so many Indian dishes, isn't really a 'curry' at all. It's a fairly dry dish, which is what the name means; dry meat. It's quite delicately spiced and nicest eaten with plain boiled rice, a cucumber, tomato and yoghurt raita and, I think, a little mango chutney. To make a feast serve it also with the Lamb Korma. You can buy prepared tamarind in jars on the spices shelf.

INGREDIENTS
Serves 4

2 tsp each ground coriander and garam masala

½ tsp chilli powder

1 onion, peeled and finely sliced

1 clove of garlic, peeled and finely chopped

55 g/2 oz ghee (clarified or cooking butter)

450 g/1 lb beef stewing steak, cut into 2.5 cm/1 in pieces

175 ml/6 fl oz tamarind water or water with the juice of a lemon mixed in

1 Mix the spices with a little water to make a thick paste.

2 Fry the onion and the garlic in the ghee or butter until lightly browned. Add the spice paste and fry it thoroughly for 2 minutes.

3 Add the meat and fry till the juices start to run. Cover with the tamarind or lemon water and simmer gently on top of the stove or in a medium to low oven, 325°F/170°C/gas mark 3, simmering oven of the Aga, for an hour and a half to two hours until it's tender and dry.

4 You may want to uncover the casserole for the last half-hour or so while it's cooking. A little chopped green coriander looks and tastes nice over the top.

DRINK RECOMMENDATION

Beer is better

Lamb and fruit kebabs

We tend to associate kebabs with Greece – clear light, wine-dark seas and a rocking bouzouki under your window at two in the morning. But in fact this recipe comes from the French colonies in the South Pacific, where there is not only a strong barbecue tradition, but plenty of exotic fruit to go with it. Fortunately for us much of that fruit is now available here on our store shelves most of the year round.

INGREDIENTS
Serves 4
Makes 1 big kebab per person

700 g/1 lb 9 oz boneless lamb, cubed

Juice and grated rind of 1 lemon

Juice and grated rind of 1 orange

Pinch of cinnamon or allspice

1 green pepper

16 pineapple cubes (fresh or tinned)

16 apricot halves or peach quarters (tinned will do)

Salt and pepper

DRINK RECOMMENDATION

Lamb is wonderful with classic reds. Try any good Claret, Burgundy or a Spanish Rioja such as

Cosme Palacio 1997 Rioja, Spain – £6.95 bottle

1 Marinate the lamb in the lemon juice and cinnamon for 2 hours.

2 De-seed the green pepper, and cut into 2.5 cm/1 in squares.

3 Using either metal or wood skewers, prepare each kebab by threading on in turn a chunk of pepper, then lamb, then pineapple, then apricot, and so on, finishing with a piece of pepper.

4 Grill or barbecue the kebabs for 3 minutes, then turn and grill for 4–5 minutes longer. Turn again and finish browning the meat.

5 Meanwhile, bring the grated rind of lemon and orange to the boil in the orange juice and simmer for 2 minutes. Add the marinade and all the other juices and season well.

6 You can thicken the sauce with a teaspoon of arrowroot used like cornflour. Serve separately with the kebabs.

Vegetarian Dishes and Vegetables

When looking for inspiration for vegetarian and vegetable dishes I once wrote that it is best to look in cuisines that are vegetarian or depend on vegetables at their heart. When choosing the dishes for this book from the hundreds that we broadcast on Classic FM I have been struck by how true this still is. The vegetarian traditions of China and India and the peasant cooking of the Mediterranean remain the best sources of inspiration.

Mark you, our own vegetable cooking has come a long way recently. We have learned not to over-cook, and to value freshness and flavour. I enjoy vegetables so much that while still a committed carnivore, I often cook two or three vegetable dishes that balance and complement each other to make up the whole meal. There are a number of recipes here that you could try that with, and one or two that are pretty well whole meals in themselves.

I can't resist adding a simple way to cook cabbage which Henry Kelly came to love. Put 1 cm/½ in of water in a stout pan, add a knob of butter and bring to the boil. Put in your washed and roughly shredded cabbage, season, put the lid on and cook for one minute. Shake vigorously, cook for only one further minute, shake again and serve. Wonderful I promise you!

Vegetarian baked beans

This is a simple adaptation of the Boston baked beans that are the ancestor of our own tinned varieties. It used to be, in its hometown, the great Saturday night dish, to be eaten with steamed molasses bread. I think we would find the original combination almost sickly sweet to our palates, so I have modified it a bit. You can, if you're not a vegetarian, add sausages or other grilled meats either into the casserole for the last half-hour or on the side, but I prefer it without.

INGREDIENTS
Serves 4

450 g/1 lb dried haricot or pinto beans, soaked for 6 hours in fresh water

Half a head of celery

1 medium sized onion

6 cloves

115 g/4 oz tomato purée

55 g/2 oz sun dried tomatoes, roughly chopped

15 g/¹/₂ oz dark soft brown sugar (known as Barbados sugar)

1 tbsp olive oil (optional)

1 Bring the beans, which have been thoroughly soaked, to the boil in the water they were soaked in. Boil for 10 minutes, strain, discard the water and cover again with fresh water to the depth of 1 cm/¹/₂ in above the surface of the beans.

2 Finely chop the celery, peel the onion, stick the cloves into it and bury it and the chopped celery in the beans. Add the tomato purée, the sun dried tomatoes and the soft brown sugar. You can also at this stage, although it isn't authentic in Massachusetts, add a tablespoon of olive oil.

3 Bring gently to the boil, cover the pot and either simmer on top of the stove or in a 180°C/350°F/gas mark 4/bottom of the Aga roasting oven for 1¹/₂ – 2 hours until the beans are completely cooked and have absorbed all the liquid. Check halfway through to make sure that all the liquid has not gone and it isn't drying out too much. On the other hand, as beans differ, if there is still a lot of liquid left at the end of the cooking time, remove the lid and boil rapidly, stirring continuously until the sauce is thickened.

4 When the beans are completely cooked, stir the mixture and remove the onion. You may remove the cloves, chop the onion and put that back if you choose. Salt the dish at this point using about a teaspoon of salt and check for the balance of sweet and saltiness and adjust if necessary. Serve with plenty of moist wholemeal bread and butter and a salad to follow.

Baked aubergines and almonds

Aubergines are now plentiful all the year round although the high season is still our summer. They originally come from the Mediterranean and so too does this dish. The combination of aubergines and almonds goes back at least to the great Arab Caliphates of the 9th and 10th centuries. Fortunately they still taste as good together today to our palates.

INGREDIENTS
Serves 4

2 medium sized aubergines (approx. 225 g/8 oz each)

75 ml/2½ fl oz olive oil

1 clove of garlic

Juice of half a lemon

25 g/1 oz finely chopped parsley

115g/4 oz white breadcrumbs

85 g/3 oz slivered almonds

1 Pre-heat the oven to 180°C/350°F/gas mark 4/bottom of the Aga roasting oven.

2 Split the aubergines in half and bake them in a greased baking dish for 45 minutes until the aubergines are soft.

3 Then, very carefully, spoon out the centre, leaving the shells, and mix the pulp with the garlic, which you've crushed with a little salt, 2 tablespoons of the olive oil, the parsley, breadcrumbs and the lemon juice. Pile the mixture back in the shells and top with the slivered almonds. Sprinkle the remaining olive oil over the top.

4 Return to the oven for 10 minutes until the almonds are just crisping.

5 Serve on its own with plenty of bread or rice or as an accompaniment to grilled kebabs.

Tortilla Valenciana

Tortillas – Spanish omelettes – are one of the great dishes of the world. They are also, though I shouldn't say it in public, a great way to use up left over bits. They are quick to make, nutritious and filling. In my house this is our usual Saturday lunch, which serves the double purpose of clearing out the fridge and providing a satisfying meal. Most things go into it OK but the eggs, potatoes and onions are essential.

INGREDIENTS
Serves 4

175 g/6 oz potatoes

175 g/6 oz onions

2 tbsp olive oil

225 g/8 oz frozen exotic mixed vegetables to include sweetcorn and red peppers

6 eggs

Plus 225 g/8 oz of anything odd left over in your fridge, cooked meat or fish, or sausage cut into small pieces

1 tsp dried herbs or 1 tbsp fresh chopped parsley, chives or marjoram.

1 Scrub, slice, then boil the potatoes until just tender – about fifteen minutes.

2 Meanwhile peel and slice the onions. Heat the oil in a big frying pan and gently fry the onions until they just start to turn golden.

3 Add the sliced potatoes, then the frozen vegetables, stir and let it cook for a minute while you beat the eggs until just frothy and then add them to the pan.

4 Mix it all together gently and cook over a medium to high heat for 2–3 minutes.

5 Now add the goodies from the fridge, meat or fish or sausage, and the herbs. The eggs should now be firm and everything else hot through.

6 Put the pan under a hot grill for 1–2 minutes until the top of the omelette is brown and bubbly. Serve in slices like a cake direct from the pan.

Monks' mixed vegetables

This dish comes from a legendary Buddhist monastery in the North of China. Buddhists of course, were strict vegetarians, we would say vegans, but the dish has a complete balance of nutrition. This is a crafty version, but one that keeps the intention of the original to be a vegetarian dish in its own right. It's best eaten as a main course served with rice.

INGREDIENTS
Serves 4

25 g/1 oz dried mushrooms

225 g/8 oz Chinese noodles

2 tbsp oil

1 tsp crushed ginger

1 small onion, peeled and sliced

½ Chinese leaf or cabbage, sliced into 1 cm/½ in ribbons

225 g/8 oz broccoli, cut into small florets

225 g/8 oz aubergines, cut in cubes

2 tbsp soy sauce

5 pieces of star anise

1 tsp sugar

1 tbsp cornflour

½ tsp cinnamon

1 block fresh tofu (white bean curd) cut into 4 matchbox size pieces

1 tbsp toasted sesame seeds

1 Put the dried mushrooms and the noodles to soak in 300 ml/½ pint of boiling hot water for 15 minutes.

2 In a deep saucepan or wok, heat the oil and fry the ginger with the onion for 3 minutes.

3 Add all the other vegetables and stir fry for 5 minutes.

4 Add the noodles, the soy sauce, star anise, sugar and the liquid the mushrooms were soaked in, and simmer for 10 minutes until everything is cooked.

5 Mix the cornflour with the cinnamon and a little water to make a smooth paste and stir it into the vegetable mixture. Bring to the boil, add the bean curd, each piece cut into four sticks, and simmer for 5 minutes.

6 Sprinkle with the toasted sesame seeds and serve.

MUSIC RECOMMENDATION

I don't know how much Buddhist and Christian monks feel they have in common. Their life styles of celibate obedience and restraint are certainly parallel, as is the Benedictine tradition of a vegetarian diet. I am therefore going to take a slight liberty and suggest, to go with a Buddhist monk's meal, the deeply calming and richly textured *Gregorian Chants* of the Benedictine monks of the monastery of Santo Domingo De Silos.

Eggs Florentine

Creamy eggs, luscious spinach and a smooth cheesy sauce all come together from one of the most sumptuous cuisines in the whole of Italy. So typical is it of the Florentine region that the French call all spinach and cheese dishes 'florentine', This is something to serve with a little Monteverdi in the background and your best Botticelli on the wall behind you. But even Blur and a British Airways calendar won't distract from the taste!

INGREDIENTS
Serves 4

4 eggs, free range for choice and flavour

25 g/1 oz butter

1 kg/2 lb 4 oz fresh spinach blanched in boiling water and well drained or 450 g/1 lb frozen spinach (thawed)

Salt and freshly ground black pepper

Pinch of ground nutmeg

4 tbsp grated Parmesan cheese

FOR THE SAUCE:

2 tbsp flour

600 ml/1 pint milk

55 g/2 oz butter

115 g/4 oz fontina or gruyère cheese

1 Put the eggs in boiling water for exactly 5 minutes, and then place in cold water. When cool, shell carefully – the yolks are still soft!

2 Melt the butter in a large pan and fry the spinach until soft and dryish.

3 To make the sauce, blend the flour with a little of the milk. Place it in a saucepan with the butter and remaining milk and bring to the boil, whisking gently until it thickens. Add the fontina or gruyère cheese and stir. Mix a third of the sauce with the cooked spinach and place in a gratin or flat baking dish. Season well with salt and pepper and sprinkle with the nutmeg.

4 Place the eggs on the spinach and cover with the remaining sauce and the Parmesan cheese. Place under a hot grill for 2 minutes only, until sizzling. Serve immediately. Wholemeal bread is nice for scraping the plates.

MUSIC RECOMMENDATION

Monteverdi is the composer who really began the modern era of classical music including composing the first real opera, 'Orpheus'. His most loved work today is his Vespers composed for the evening church services in Mantua in 1610.

Lemon and almond rice

If I want to impress at a big party this is one of the dishes that top my list. Good enough to eat on its own with some salad, this delicate rice dish is speckled with green from the parsley and looks wonderful. It's also easy to make and acts as an excellent background for anything from poached salmon to Thai chicken.

INGREDIENTS
This recipe makes enough for a buffet, serving up to 14 people

225 g/8 oz blanched almonds

700 g/1 lb 9 oz long grain or basmati rice, rinsed

2 tsp salt

25 g/1 oz fresh parsley

450 g/1 lb oyster or chestnut mushrooms, washed and sliced

2 tbsp sunflower oil

115 g/4 oz butter

Grated rind and juice of 3 lemons

Seasoning

1 Toast the almonds in a hot dry frying pan until they are golden brown. Remove from the pan and set them aside.

2 Cook the rice in plenty of boiling water with the salt for 10–12 minutes until the rice is just cooked and tender. You will probably find it best to do this in 2 large pans rather than all at once in a huge one. Drain thoroughly and rinse through with hot water and drain again.

3 Finely chop the parsley and slice the mushrooms thinly. Heat the oil and butter in 2 large frying pans and fry the mushrooms for 2–3 minutes until they are a little softened.

4 Add the almonds and rice to the pan and stir until the rice is warmed through, and buttery. Then add the parsley, lemon rind and the juice, check the seasoning and serve hot or at room temperature.

Brown rice pilau

Try brown rice for a change, it has a nutty taste and a slightly chewy texture. In fact it's not a lot better for you than white rice, having very little extra fibre or minerals, but it does taste good, particularly in robust dishes like this one. This recipe can be eaten as a meal in itself or served alongside other dishes.

INGREDIENTS
Serves 4

225 g/8 oz Spanish onion

2 garlic cloves

225 g/8 oz carrots

225 g/8 oz courgettes

2 tbsp olive oil

450 g/1 lb brown basmati rice, rinsed under cold running water

900 ml/1½ pints vegetable stock

55 g/2 oz slivered almonds, toasted (you can buy them like this)

25 g/1 oz chopped fresh parsley

Seasoning

Bowl of thick Greek yoghurt, to serve

1 Peel the onion and garlic. Fine chop the garlic and cut the onion into 5 mm/¼ in dice. Peel the carrots and cut them into the same sized pieces. Trim the courgettes and dice likewise.

2 Heat the oil in a pan big enough to take all the ingredients. Fry the garlic gently, add the onion and the carrots and cook for 5 minutes. Add the rice and turn until thoroughly coated. Add the stock, season generously, bring to the boil, turn down and cover and cook for 20 minutes. Add the chopped courgettes onto the top of the rice, which by now should be pretty nearly dry, and allow to cook for another 5 minutes over a very low heat.

3 To serve: turn the pilau, which should be just moist but have no free liquid in it, onto a serving platter and sprinkle with almonds and parsley. A bowl of yoghurt goes very nicely at the side of this.

Opposite: ***Lemon and almond rice***
Brown rice pilau

New potato, broad bean and mushroom gratin

By happy coincidence new potatoes and broad beans are at their best at the same time of year. This is a great gift because their flavours complement each other perfectly and make a marvellous and nutritionally balanced vegetarian gratin. This can be eaten as a course or dish on its own or served with simple grilled meats or fish if that's your inclination.

INGREDIENTS
Serves 4

350 g/12 oz new potatoes

350 g/12 oz broad beans, podded

115 g/4 oz chestnut or shitaki mushrooms

225 g/8 oz fromage frais (8% fat)

2 eggs

55 g/2 oz grated pecorino or parmesan cheese

115 g/4 oz fresh white breadcrumbs

1 Pre-heat the oven to 200°C/400°F/gas mark 6/top of the Aga roasting oven.

2 Scrub and boil the potatoes until they're just tender, about 10 minutes. Remove from the water and drain. Use the water to boil the broad beans for 5 minutes. Scald the mushrooms by pouring a kettle of boiling water over them in a colander in the sink. Cut into quarters.

3 Cut the potatoes in half and mix all the drained vegetables together. Put them into a buttered gratin dish into which all the ingredients will just fit. Spoon over the fromage frais, which you have mixed with the beaten eggs and sprinkle with the grated cheese and breadcrumbs mixed together.

4 Bake for 20 minutes until the topping is lightly golden.

DRINK RECOMMENDATION

A crisp, dry white.
Touraine Sauvignon Blanc
1998 – £3.99

Chinese chilli cabbage

This dish, originally from China, has been adopted all over South East Asia with some variants. You can make it with almost any kind of cabbage: it's equally successful with one of the crisp Dutch ones normally sold for coleslaw, or with one of the Chinese style pale green celery cabbages. It's okay too with the crinkly, coarse leafed Savoy we get in the winter. Adjust the volume of chilli and garlic to your own taste and to the strength of the cabbage's flavour. The important thing is to make sure that the leaves are still crisp and have some bite to them when you've finished cooking.

INGREDIENTS
Serves 4

450 g/1 lb crisp cabbage

2 tbsp oil

2 cloves of garlic

1 tbsp (or to taste) Chinese style, thick, sweet chilli sauce

$\frac{1}{2}$ tsp salt

1 Shred the cabbage across the grain into 5 mm/$\frac{1}{4}$ in slices removing any core or solid pieces.

2 Heat the oil in a wok or a large frying pan. Peel and crush the garlic and add that to the oil. Fry for 30 seconds and add the cabbage.

3 Stir and toss for 2 minutes until the cabbage is coated with the garlic oil and beginning to soften. Add the chilli sauce and half a cup of water. Cover for 30 seconds for the cabbage to steam. Season with salt and serve immediately. There should be very little liquid left in the bottom; what liquid there is should not be served with the cabbage.

Spiced roast potatoes

This is a revelation. Even people who don't like spicy food can't get enough of potatoes cooked like this, so while the quantities I give you are those for 6 people under normal circumstances, you may find it's only enough for four when they've tasted them. Do make sure your oven is hot enough to crisp the potatoes. If you are cooking anything big in it at the same time, the temperature will inevitably drop.

INGREDIENTS
Serves 6

900 g/2 lb potatoes, peeled and cut into quarters (Desirée are a good variety for this)

2 large garlic cloves, crushed

1 tsp salt

2 tbsp chilli purée or thick chilli sauce

4 tbsp vegetable oil

1 Pre-heat the oven to 200°C/400°F/gas mark 4/top of the Aga roasting oven.

2 Put the potatoes into a pan of cold salted water, bring to the boil and simmer for 6 minutes. Drain thoroughly. Mix the crushed garlic and salt with the chilli paste and coat the potatoes with it thoroughly. Leave for 10 minutes for the flavours to develop.

3 Heat the oil in a roasting tin, turn the potatoes in the oil and roast for 45 minutes until cooked through and golden brown.

Spinach with sesame seed dressing

This is a dish from Japan where spinach is often eaten cold, something I've never experienced anywhere else. As with so much in Japanese food it is unexpectedly absolutely delicious. Spinach like this is surprisingly substantial and very appealing to the Western palate. It's eaten as part of a range of dishes in a Japanese meal with three or four other specialities to balance it. I like it as a side dish or instead of a salad or as a starter. It can be made quite a long time in advance providing you don't add the dressing until the last moment. The ingredients are readily available.

INGREDIENTS
Serves 4

700 g/1 lb 9 oz fresh leaf spinach

Juice of half a lemon

1 tsp salt

4 tbsp sesame paste (tahini)

2 tsp sesame oil

2 tsp soy sauce

1 Wash and trim the spinach leaves and put them to boil for 3 minutes in a saucepan full of boiling water. Drain thoroughly in a colander and chop them up with a knife in the colander to allow any excess liquid to drain off. You should then have a block of spinach about the size of a saucer and about 1–2 cm/$\frac{1}{2}$–$\frac{3}{4}$ in thick.

2 Allow to cool and shape it into an oblong about the size of two large matchboxes. These oblongs can be divided up into 4 portions similar in shape but smaller in size, one for each diner.

3 Mix the sauce ingredients together, the sesame paste and oil with the lemon juice and the salt. If the tahini is particularly thick you may find that heating it in a saucepan with a tablespoon or two of water will help blend it all together better. If you do heat it, allow it to cool before spooning the sauce onto each of the portions of spinach.

4 You can make the spinach up to 12 hours before and keep it in the fridge. Sauce it only half an hour before, otherwise it loses its particularly attractive appearance and contrast between the pale sauce and the dark green spinach.

Puddings and Bakes

Puddings: everybody's favourite course, unless you are on a diet that is. If you are, then pudding is not a matter of favourite, but fantasy. In fact most of my puddings are based on fruit in its many wonderful forms, so while they can be quite rich and filling, they are not in the 'death by chocolate' category.

We are born, it seems, with a sweet tooth and so our liking for the last course is only natural. Included here is a selection of our Friday recipes. 'At last' Henry would proclaim at around half past ten every Friday morning, 'Puddin' day'. A more reliable forecast I'm bound to say than his horseracing tips.

When it comes to baking, my sort is the crafty sort. There are few smells more delightful than an oven full of bread or pastries and few things nicer to eat. BUT, and as you can see it's a big 'but', I don't want to spend hours in the kitchen getting to that point. So over the years I have devised a number of short cuts and simple ways to achieve some quite spectacular results.

These were also broadcast on our 'Pudding' spot whether or not the dish was meant to be eaten as a pud. Both Henry Kelly and I as children had been raised in the High Tea tradition, in our Irish and Welsh backgrounds respectively. In that pattern of eating the main evening meal is taken around six o'clock, when the foods normally associated with tea time…bread and butter and jam and cake and pastries… are expanded with a cooked but simple dish like kippers or smoked haddock or potato cakes and sausages, with perhaps a salad in the summer. It's a very attractive way of eating if your life style fits, and many of these recipes suit it perfectly.

Lemon syllabub

Syllabub is an old English formulation, originally made with milk still hot from the cow. Today we have to make do with double cream! It is a marvellous, creamy, lemony pudding and very rich. In Victorian times they decorated this with whipped or even clotted cream. You can do this if you like, but the modern taste for lighter food suggests leaving well enough alone.

INGREDIENTS
Serves 4

300 ml/½ pint double cream

Grated rind and juice of 2 lemons, preferably unwaxed

175 ml/6 fl oz freshly squeezed orange juice

85 g/3 oz caster sugar

1 Lightly beat the cream until it is thick. In a separate bowl, mix the lemon and orange juice with the caster sugar, and then whisk this into the cream, a little at a time, so the juice is completely absorbed before you add more.

2 Add the grated lemon rind, stir it into the cream and spoon the mixture into four attractive glasses. You can decorate them with a thin slice of lemon, if you like.

3 Leave it to set in the fridge for at least 2 hours until it is like a firm mousse. It may separate a little. You can leave the syllabub covered in the fridge for up to 24 hours. Crispy biscuits like lemon thins are nice with this.

Old English custard tart with bay

This is a wonderful pudding. It is easy to make, quite light to eat if it is made well, and very comforting. You need either shortcrust pastry or pâté sablée (see page 108 for the recipe) – shortcrust made with an egg instead of water. In England the tradition of making mixed fat pie pastry (white fat and butter) goes back a long way and has much to recommend it. Today I would urge vegetarian white fat rather than saturated lard. You can buy ready-made pastry, which is surprisingly good.

INGREDIENTS
Serves 4
with second helpings

225 g/8 oz shortcrust pastry or pâté sablée

2 eggs +1 yolk

150 ml/¼ pint full-cream milk or single cream

3–4 tbsp caster sugar

2 bay leaves

1 tsp ground nutmeg, preferably freshly grated

1 This was originally made in a china tart plate, but it cooks much better in a tin or aluminium one, which gives a crisper finish to the pastry. That's important as the filling is quite runny. You need a 20 cm/8 in tin.

2 Pre-heat the oven to 220°C/425°F/gas mark 7/very top of the Aga roasting oven.

3 Either roll out the pastry and line the tin with it, or, as I do, knuckle it into the tin until it is spread out. Run a fork over the top to make sure it is nice and neat. Whisk the eggs, the milk and the sugar together until they are thoroughly mixed, and pour it through a sieve into the pastry case. The sieve is essential to make sure it works properly.

4 Put the bay leaves into the mixture. Sprinkle the nutmeg on top and bake it for about 35 minutes in a hot oven. After about 25 minutes check to make sure the pastry isn't burning, and the custard isn't cooking too quickly. You may need to turn the heat down just a bit to about 200°C/400°F/gas mark 6. Try to avoid opening the oven door too much as the tart will have risen quite a lot and the more you open it the more it sinks.

5 When it is cooked, turn off the heat, but leave the tart in the oven for five minutes with the door shut. If you have an Aga move it to the slow oven. Then put it in a draught free place and let it cool. Don't eat it straight away, it needs to set a bit. I like to let it cool gently and eat it cold when it has a wonderful creamy texture.

Gooseberry and elderflower fool

With gooseberries at the right time of year, come their counterpart, elderflowers. These can be picked all over the place on waste ground if you don't happen to have any in your garden. They're used to flavour all sorts of things but mixed with gooseberries they provide the most extraordinary muscat flavour normally only found in the most expensive grapes. You can at a pinch use elderflower cordial, which is now widely sold. This fool is very easy to make and has a refreshing sharpness as well as richness to it.

INGREDIENTS
Serves 4

450 g/1 lb gooseberries, topped and tailed

140 g/5 oz caster sugar

1 head elderflower blossoms or 1 tbsp elderflower cordial

300 ml/¹/₂ pint whipping cream

1 Put the gooseberries with the sugar into a non-stick saucepan with just a tablespoon or two of water to help them start to cook. Cook gently until the gooseberries begin to break up.

2 Add the carefully washed head of elderflowers and crush it into the mixture (do not add cordial at this stage). Simmer for 10 to 15 minutes until the gooseberries are cooked through.

3 Remove and discard the elderflower and either purée or thoroughly mash the gooseberry mixture.

4 Add the elderflower cordial now if using it.

5 Whip the cream until it's thick and fold carefully into the gooseberry mixture so that they're thoroughly mixed. Place in a serving bowl or in individual soufflé dishes or cups. Chill for 2 hours before serving.

MUSIC RECOMMENDATION

No one has ever explained the name 'fool' for an English cream and fruit pudding to my satisfaction but it does give me the chance to suggest a piece of music with connections to the name. Fools play quite a part in the mythology of 19th century classical music; Pagliacci for example or the eponymous tragic hero of Rigoletto. My favourite is I think *Petrushka,* Stravinsky's tragicomic ballet score for the legendary Ballets Russes of Diaghilev written at the beginning of this century.

French fruit tart

If you are short of time, you can use bought shortcrust pastry for this classic French recipe, but pâté sablée is better. It is a more crumbly and sweeter pastry than shortcrust, and is easier to roll out thinly. It doesn't take long to make, especially in a food processor. The fruit you use is really whatever you fancy. Pears, peaches, apricots, plums or apples are all delicious at different times of year.

INGREDIENTS
Serves 4

FOR THE PÂTÉ SABLÉE:

115 g/4 oz plain flour

70 g/2½ oz butter

½ tsp salt

1 egg yolk

25 g/1 oz caster sugar

1–2 tbsp cold water

FOR THE FILLING:

900 g/2 lb fruit

4 tbsp apricot jam

4 tbsp water

1 You can make the pastry either by hand or in a food processor. Mix together the flour, butter and salt and caster sugar until the mixture resembles fine breadcrumbs. Add the egg yolk and then the water, ½ teaspoon at a time, until the pastry binds together. If you're making it by hand, you may need a little less water than if you are using a food processor. Either way, when it is made, press it firmly with the heel of your hand, wrap it in clingfilm and chill for 30 minutes before using.

2 Pre-heat the oven to 200°C/400°F/gas mark 6/middle of the Aga roasting oven. And grease a 20 cm/8 in flan tin.

3 Core or stone the fruit, depending on what it is, but don't peel it. Slice it thinly.

4 Roll out the pastry and line the flan tin with it. Put a piece of foil in the middle to weigh it down and bake in the oven for 10 minutes. Take it out, remove the foil and put the pastry back in the oven for another 5 minutes to let it dry out. It should be a pale biscuity gold colour all over. Remove and let it cool.

5 Arrange the slices of fruit on the pastry in neat overlapping rows. Melt the apricot jam and water together and brush over the fruit to glaze. Put the fruit-filled pastry in the hot oven for 15 to 20 minutes, making sure it doesn't burn at the edges.

6 You can serve it hot, though in France it is more usually allowed to cool.

DRINK RECOMMENDATION

Try a lovely chilled glass of Beaumes-de-Venise, with its grapey, fruity, apricot freshness.

Muscat de Beaumes-de-Venise France – £4.99 half bottle

Peaches baked in honey and lemon

This recipe takes, literally, just minutes to prepare and only seems to last a couple of seconds at the table. It tastes as lovely as it sounds. I should cook it more often!

INGREDIENTS
Serves 4

4 ripe peaches or
1 x 400 g/14 oz can peach halves in natural juice

8 cardamom pods

15 g/¹/₂ oz sugar

1¹/₂ tbsp clear honey

Juice and rind of
¹/₂ lemon

125 ml/4 fl oz white grape juice

Crème fraîche, to serve

1 Pre-heat the oven to 200°C/400°F/gas mark 6/top of the Aga roasting oven.

2 If using fresh peaches, place them in a pan of boiling water and leave for 1 minute. Remove with a slotted spoon and drain on kitchen paper. Peel, cut in half and remove the stones.

3 Arrange the fresh or canned peach halves in a large ovenproof dish, cut side up. Lightly bruise the cardamom pods and put one in each peach.

4 To make the syrup, place the sugar, honey, lemon juice and rind in a small pan and add the grape juice. Bring to the boil and simmer for 1–2 minutes until the sugar has dissolved. Pour over the peach halves and bake for 20–25 minutes, basting occasionally.

5 Serve at once with a bowl of crème fraîche, or let the peaches cool in their syrup.

Lemon meringue pie

This is one of the great pies of America and is made in a variety of different forms. In particular the thickness of the filling and meringue topping varies greatly. In every aspect except flavour this version leans towards the moderate. The recipe is derived from a classic New England method and produces a very lemony and very rich pie.

INGREDIENTS
Serves 6

350 g/12 oz shortcrust pastry

4 tbsp cornflour

425 ml/³/₄ pint boiling water

¹/₂ tsp salt

225 g/8 oz caster sugar

1 tbsp butter

Grated rind and juice of 3 lemons

4 eggs, separated

1 Pre-heat the oven to 200°C/400°F/gas mark 6/middle of the Aga roasting oven.

2 Roll out the pastry and use to line a 23 cm/9 in deep flan dish, if you like you can bake it 'blind' first. You could also use a ready-made sweet pastry case.

3 Stir about 1 tablespoon of water into the cornflour and mix until smooth, then stir it into the boiling water, off the heat, along with the salt and half of the sugar. Put in a bowl over a saucepan of boiling water and whisk until the whole lot comes to the boil. Simmer for 15 minutes, stirring gently. If you have a heavy non-stick saucepan, you can do this carefully over direct heat.

4 Take the bowl off the heat and beat in the tablespoon of butter and the lemon juice and rind. Stir in the egg yolks and mix thoroughly. Use this mixture to fill the pastry shell.

5 In a separate bowl, beat the egg whites vigorously until stiff, gradually adding the rest of the sugar. Spoon the meringue onto the pie and bake until the meringue is golden. This should take about 25–30 minutes.

6 Leave to cool a little before serving, or serve cold.

DRINK RECOMMENDATION

A glass of fresh sweet lemonade

Fruit and meringue torrone

This pudding is a delicious frozen concoction of meringues and cream topped with raspberries. Although it's not an ice cream in the conventional sense, it is one of those Italian confections that have given 'gelati' such a good name. It makes an elegant end to a summer meal. When serving it use a sharp knife dipped into hot water between each slice. It will make things much easier.

INGREDIENTS
Serves 6–8

8 individual meringue nests or half shells of meringue (shop-bought or home made)

425 ml/15 fl oz double cream

2 tbsp Amaretto liqueur or ½ tsp good vanilla essence

Icing sugar, to taste

Oil, for greasing, not olive

225 g/8 oz raspberries, thawed if frozen

25 g/1 oz caster sugar

Icing sugar, to dust

Tiny mint sprigs, to garnish

1 Break each half-shell of meringue into bite-sized pieces and place in a large bowl. Lightly whip the cream in a separate bowl and gently fold in the Amaretto or vanilla essence then sweeten with icing sugar – about a tablespoonful.

2 Tip the cream mixture into the meringues and stir just enough to mix. Use a pastry brush to oil a 1.2 ml/2 pint loaf tin and fill with the meringue and cream mixture, smoothing down the top. Wipe down the edges to clean and freeze for at least 2 hours or up to 1 week.

3 Dip the mould in warm water and turn out on to a plate. Mix the raspberries with the caster sugar and leave while you cut the torrone into slices and serve with a spoonful of raspberries on top and a dusting of icing sugar, garnishing with the mint sprigs.

MUSIC RECOMMENDATION

To eat with an Italian ice cream-like dish there can only be one choice and that is what's known as the Wall's Ice Cream Song from its use in those (and other) TV commercials. In fact *O Sole Mio* is only one of a series of Neapolitan traditional songs orchestrated in the late 19th century as a showcase for theatrical tenors and performed and recorded by them ever since. You can take your pick of performers, but one of the earliest recorded versions is by Caruso and is still magical despite the scratches.

Fresh cream strawberry tarts

Strawberry tarts are not only delicious to eat but they must be the prettiest thing to look at. If we eat with our eyes, as the saying goes, these are a feast on a plate. You can buy small boat-shaped pastry moulds to make individual tarts, though it works fine in a conventional round tart tin. Like the French Fruit Tart, this is better made with pâté sablée rather than shortcrust pastry. (See page 108 for the recipe.)

INGREDIENTS
Serves 4

FOR THE FILLING:

3 tbsp double cream

3 tbsp fromage frais

450 g/1 lb strawberries, hulled

115 g/4 oz strawberry jam

4 tbsp water

1 tbsp lemon juice

1 Pre-heat the oven 200°C/400°F/gas mark 6/top of the Aga roasting oven.

2 Roll out the pastry and line a 20 cm/8 in tart tin with it. Put a piece of foil in the middle and fill it with dried beans if you have some. Bake it in the oven for 12–15 minutes. Take the foil out and continue to bake for another 5 minutes until the pastry is a lovely pale gold colour. Take out of the oven and allow to cool.

3 Whip the double cream until thick and fold in the fromage frais. Spoon a thick layer of the cream mixture into the pastry case. If the strawberries are large, slice them, and pile as many as you comfortably can on top of the cream. Melt the strawberry jam with the water and lemon juice and beat until smooth. When it is cool, trickle it over the top so it runs down between the strawberries. Make sure none of the strawberries are left uncovered by the glaze.

4 Allow a few moments for it to set, and serve. Once made, it will not keep long – the pastry will go soggy in the fridge – but you can prepare it all ahead and simply fill the pastry case up to an hour before you sit down to eat.

Mixed berry shortcake

Although strawberry shortcake has always seemed to me an American invention, this version comes from Denmark where the unsalted butter that makes it so delicious is also produced. The mixture makes wonderful biscuits, too, treated slightly differently as I've indicated below. This makes a cake using mixed summer berries though you can just use strawberries if you prefer.

INGREDIENTS
Serves 4–6

175 g/6 oz unsalted butter

225 g/8 oz self-raising flour, sifted

85 g/3 oz caster sugar

FOR THE FILLING AND TOPPING:

225 g/8 oz mixed berries such as raspberries, blueberries or blackberries

150 ml/¹/₄ pint double cream (or half each double cream and yoghurt), whipped

1 Pre-heat the oven to 200°C/400°F/gas mark 6/top of Aga roasting oven.

2 Make sure that the butter is soft. Mix it with the flour and sugar to a stiff dough. Press into an 18 cm/7 in cake tin, level the top, then prick all over with a fork. Bake for 20 minutes, keeping an eye on it. If the top starts to brown too soon, cover it with a piece of buttered paper.

3 Turn the cake out onto a wire rack and, whilst still warm but not hot, carefully split in half horizontally. Leave to cool, then sandwich together with half the fruits and cream, whipped till it is thick. Repeat on top of the cake, decorating it with the best whole fruit.

Variation: Press the mixture into a Swiss roll tin, divide into 5 cm/2 in oblongs and decorate with pieces of almond or cherries. Bake for 15 minutes only and you have really delicious shortbread.

Pear and almond frangipani

This is a French-style pastry with a double filling. You can use tinned pears at a pinch, but it's much better to peel, halve, core and poach your own for about 10 minutes in a syrup made from 115 g/4 oz sugar and 300 ml/½ pint water. The tart is very spectacular and should be served with a whole pear half in the centre of each slice.

INGREDIENTS
Serves 8

FOR THE PASTRY:

225 g/8 oz plain flour

2 tbsp caster sugar

115 g/4 oz butter, well chilled

Pinch of salt

1 egg

FOR THE FILLING:

55 g/2 oz butter

55 g/2 oz caster sugar

55 g/2 oz ground almonds

25 g/1 oz self-raising flour

½ tsp almond essence

1 egg

3 tbsp milk

4 pears, as 8 pear halves, cored, poached and cooled

1 Pre-heat the oven to 220°C/425°F/gas mark 7/top of the Aga roasting oven

2 You can make the pastry by hand or in a food processor. If you're using a processor, put all the pastry ingredients, except the egg, in together. Then add the egg and – gradually – enough water for the dough to form a ball around the blade of the processor. By hand, work the flour, caster sugar and butter together with the salt until the mixture resembles fine breadcrumbs. Work in the egg and a little water until the pastry clings firmly. Knead briefly, roll it into a ball and allow it to rest in the fridge for 30 minutes before using.

3 Thinly roll out the pastry on a lightly floured surface. Use to line a 25 cm/10 in tart tin. Cream the butter and sugar together for the frangipani. Add the remaining ingredients except the pears and mix together. Fill the pastry case with the mixture. Place the poached pear halves on top like spokes of a wheel, pointed ends to the middle, then bake for 30–35 minutes until the pastry is crisp and the pears are tender and the frangipani filling is risen and golden.

4 Serve either warm or cold.

MUSIC RECOMMENDATION

I have no real reason to put this dish and the music that follows together but I do have two excuses. Firstly I haven't recommended any Mozart yet, and secondly both the piece and the pie are amongst my favourites. Mozart wrote lots of music to eat and party to, called Divertimenti, but I'm going to suggest something to really listen to while you savour your frangipani – the Piano Sonata in *A major K 331*. If you can persuade Murray Perahia to play it for you, it would be bliss.

Spiced apple and raisin filo

This is a really quick and easy recipe. You will need to stew your own apples with some brown sugar, cinnamon and raisins to make this dish. I always do lots using either windfalls or bramleys (or both) as it never lasts long in my fridge, being eaten from breakfast onwards. Do leave enough to make this lovely light pastry though.

INGREDIENTS
Serves 4

6 sheets filo pastry, thawed if frozen

85 g/3 oz melted butter

55 g/2 oz fresh white breadcrumbs

100 g/3½ oz flaked almonds

400 g/14 oz stewed apple with raisins

A little icing sugar, for dusting

1 Pre-heat the oven to 180°C/350°F/gas mark 4/ bottom of the Aga roasting oven

2 Place one sheet of filo pastry in a 18 cm/7 in square baking tin and brush with a little melted butter and sprinkle over half of the breadcrumbs. Place a second sheet on top, brush with a little of the butter and sprinkle over 25 g/1 oz of the almonds.

3 Spoon half the fruit filling on top. Repeat the layers and finish with a double layer of filo. Brush with the remaining melted butter and sprinkle the rest of the almonds on top. Lightly score the top with a sharp knife to make a criss-cross pattern and bake for 30 minutes until crisp and golden.

4 Dust with the icing sugar and serve either warm or cold cut into squares.

DRINK RECOMMENDATION

A raisiny sun-dried wine is in its element here. Try this Italian delight:

Passito di Pantelleria DOC 1997 Pellegrino – £5.95 half bottle

Pineapple and coconut bake

This dish is derived from a Caribbean recipe where there is a tradition of quite substantial and sweet baking with the local ingredients, particularly coconut. This has a shortcake base and a delicious soft centred macaroon-type topping.

INGREDIENTS
Serves 8

FOR THE BASE:

225 g/8 oz plain flour

115 g/4 oz soft brown sugar

175 g/6 oz butter

FOR THE MIXTURE:

4 eggs

225 g/8 oz caster sugar

55 g/2 oz plain flour

½ tsp baking powder

½ tsp salt

½ tsp cinnamon

225 g/8 oz pineapple pieces, tinned or fresh

115 g/4 oz desiccated coconut

55 g/2 oz chopped mixed nuts

1 tsp vanilla essence

115 g/4 oz glacé cherries

1 Pre-heat the oven to 350°F/180°C/gas mark 4/bottom of the Aga roasting oven.

2 To make the base, mix the flour and sugar and rub in the butter.

3 Press into the bottom of a 20 cm–23 cm/8 or 9 in spring-form cake tin. Bake for 20 minutes. Turn down the oven to 300°F/150°C/gas mark 2/Aga simmering oven.

4 Beat the eggs in a large bowl and add the caster sugar; whisk until thick, pale and light. Placing the bowl over a saucepan of simmering water will quicken the process. (If using an electric mixer no heat is required.) When thick, remove from the heat and whisk until cool. Lightly fold in the flour, baking powder, salt and cinnamon.

5 Drain the pineapple pieces and add to the mixture with the coconut, nuts and vanilla and mix well. Lay the cherries on top of the base, cover with the mixture and bake for 1 hour 15 minutes. This bake is good hot or cold, and can be re-heated in a moderate oven.

6 Serve on its own or with custard or vanilla ice cream.

Apple and sultana cake

With origins in the West Country, here is a particularly scrumptious and juicy cake with a strong fruit content. You can treat it as a fruitcake but I like it on picnics as it seems especially nice to eat in the open air.

INGREDIENTS
Serves 4–6

200 g/7 oz softened butter

140 g/5 oz caster sugar

225 g/8 oz self-raising flour

1½ tsp baking powder

2 large eggs

Juice and grated rind of 1 lemon

1–2 tbsp milk (optional)

450 g/1 lb eating apples, peeled and cored, about 3 in total

85 g/3 oz sultanas

1 Pre-heat the oven to 190°C/375°F/gas mark 5/bottom of the Aga roasting oven.

2 You can use a food processor for this recipe. If you are making the cake by hand you have to use the creaming method beginning with the butter and the sugar and then adding the flour, baking powder, eggs and lemon rind and juice separately.

If using a food processor, put all the ingredients except the apples and sultanas in and blend to a smooth paste. If the mixture is too stiff, add a tablespoon or two (not more) of milk.

3 Cut the apples into small dice, add in the sultanas and mix half into the cake mixture. Pour half of it into a greased 20 cm/8 in cake tin, add the remaining chopped apple and sultanas and cover with the remaining cake mixture. Cover loosely with a piece of foil and bake in the oven for about 1 hour until risen and firm to the touch.

4 Test with a skewer, which should come out clean if the cake is cooked. If not, allow another 10 minutes or so. Cool and serve from the tin. It's not a spectacularly high cake in terms of rising but is wonderfully moist and succulent.

Opposite: ***Apple and sultana cake***
Banana bread

Banana bread

This is a sort of loaf that can be eaten as a cake on its own or spread with butter and treated rather like an exotic form of malt loaf. It's very rich though, and I'm not totally sure that the buttered version is that good for your health, although it is very good to eat.

INGREDIENTS
Serves 6

3 ripe bananas

115 g/4 oz soft brown sugar

115 g/4 oz butter or margarine

225 g/8 oz self raising flour

2 eggs

4 tbsp milk

115 g/4 oz sultanas

1 Pre-heat the oven to 200°C/400°F/gas mark 6/middle of the Aga roasting oven.

2 Peel the bananas and mash them thoroughly.

3 Cream the soft brown sugar and butter together (this can be done in a processor if you wish). Add the flour, the mashed banana, the eggs and the milk and work together thoroughly until a coherent batter is achieved. It should be the thickness of moderately whipped cream, still capable of falling off the spoon. If it's too thick, add a couple more tablespoons of milk as bananas vary in size, and flour varies in its capacity to absorb liquid.

4 When it's floppy but still coherent stir in the sultanas and put the mixture into a buttered loaf tin, a 900 g/2 lb tin should be the right size, and bake for about 45 to 50 minutes. You may need to cover the top of it towards the end of this time to prevent it burning. Check to see if it's done by inserting a skewer. The skewer should come out clean. If it's still smeary, put the loaf back in for another 5 to 6 minutes' cooking.

5 When it's done, take it out and turn it out onto a rack as soon as it's cool enough to handle. It's got to be left to cool before you eat it. Slice it like a loaf, I think you'll enjoy the combination of texture and flavour.

Chocolate gâteau

This can only be described as a serious chocolate cake and it is unbelievably easy to make. To make you feel slightly less guilty about eating it, it is made with polyunsaturated oil, not with saturated fats like butter. The method sounds deeply unlikely. All I can say is, trust me!

INGREDIENTS
Serves 6

175 g/6 oz self-raising flour

4 heaped tbsp of real cocoa powder

1 heaped tsp of baking powder

115 g/4 oz caster sugar

2 tsp black treacle

150 ml/¹⁄₄ pint sunflower oil

150 ml/¹⁄₄ pint milk

2 large eggs

1 Pre-heat the oven to 170°C/325°F/gas mark 3/top of the Aga simmering oven.

2 You can either make this by hand in a large basin or let a food processor do it for you. Put every single ingredient into whichever you are using and either beat it very well with a wooden spoon, or give it a whiz until the mixture is smooth, dark brown and creamy.

3 Pour it into 2 x 18 cm/7 in greased and lined sandwich tins. Loose bottoms and non-stick make this even easier to do, though you should still grease and line them. Bake for 45 minutes. You may want to put a sheet of greaseproof paper over them so they do not cook too fast. Test by pressing the top gently; if it comes back•with a bounce it's cooked, if it stays down, it needs another five minutes.

4 Allow the cakes to cool, then turn them out. You can now fill the cake with all sorts of things. I suggest apricot jam spread in the middle, sandwiching the two halves together with a little fromage frais on the top as a kind of frosting. You can, of course, use black cherry jam and whipped double cream and do the whole Black Forest number. I leave it to you and your bathroom scales!

Sunflower seed bread

Wholemeal breads are often quite heavy and overly chewable, especially when home-made. I think you will find this one more palatable while retaining bags of flavour and quite a firm texture. While the recipe takes a couple of hours, only about 15 minutes of that is your time, particularly if you have an oven with a timed bake facility.

INGREDIENTS

350 g/12 oz wholemeal bread flour

1 pkt ready mix yeast

½ tsp salt

175 ml/6 fl oz warm water

1 tbsp golden syrup or runny honey

2 tbsp oil

85 g/3 oz peeled sunflower seeds

1 Mix the flour with the yeast and salt in a big bowl. Mix the water, oil and honey together and pour over the flour.

2 Knead together for a couple of minutes until the mixture changes texture and becomes an elastic dough. You can do this in a mixer or processor if you like. Leave it in a warm place to rise, covered with a clean cloth, for about 50 minutes.

3 Knead again adding the sunflower seeds and put into a medium loaf tin and leave to rise for about 40 minutes.

4 Bake in a hot oven 220°C/425°F/gas mark 7/top of the Aga roasting oven, for 45 minutes.

5 Tip out of the tin and test by knocking on the base. If it sounds hollow it's done. If not switch off the oven and give it another 7 minutes. Cool before eating. It improves if left overnight.

Index

numbers in italics refer to illustrations